AN UNSENTIMENTAL JOURNEY

THROUGH CORNWALL

An
Unsentimental Journey
Through
Cornwall

by The Author of "John Halifax, Gentleman"
Illustrated by C. Napier Hemy

with a Foreword by Professor Charles Thomas
Director, Institute of Cornish Studies
University of Exeter
and
Bibliographic Memoir by Dr. Melissa Hardie
The Jamieson Library of Women's History

Newmill, Penzance
The Jamieson Library
1988

An edition published for
The Jamieson Library in 1988
Newmill, Penzance, Cornwall
by the Patten Press
66 Hayle Terrace
Hayle, Cornwall TR27 4BT
Printed in Great Britain by
Dotesios Press, Bradford on Avon

First published in 1884 by
Macmillan and Co., London.
Printed by R. Clay, Sons and Taylor
Bread Street Hill, E.C.

Cover design by Carole Page
Foreword by Charles Thomas
Memoir by Melissa Hardie

British Library Cataloguing in Publication Data
Craik, Dinah Maria Muloch
An Unsentimental Journey Through Cornwall
1. Craik, Dinah M.M. 2.Travel - Cornwall
I. Title II. Hardie, Melissa

ISBN 0 9507689 6 0

ST. MICHAEL'S MOUNT.

FOREWORD

FOR too many years *An Unsentimental Journey Through Cornwall* has been a rarity, and an expensive rarity, in booksellers' catalogues, and several generations of enthusiasts for Cornish literature have been deprived of the joy of reading it. Its re-issue cannot be too warmly welcomed, and in case the slightly coy anonymity on the title page confuses the modern reader, the authoress of *John Halifax, Gentleman* (first published in 1856 as a three-decker) was Mrs. Dinah Mulock Craik. A brief acquaintance with the tone and substance of either *An Unsentimental Journey,* or *John Halifax,* is enough to suggest that Mrs. Craik was an extremely competent writer and a most attractive personality. She was born in 1826 (20 April) at Stoke-on-Trent, where her father the Reverend Thomas Mulock was minister of a small congregation, and in 1864, she married George Lillie Craik, who was a partner in the London publishing house of Macmillan's. Mrs. Craik had a North country hold upon reality, was renowned for her business acumen, and at one point could command the astonishing figure of £2000 for the copyright of a story.

A prolific author, Mrs. Craik left nearly forty novels and a fair selection of poetry, *belles lettres* and literary comment. She also published translations from the French. After her death (from heart failure, 12 October, 1887), the notices that her work attracted included a particular appreciation from Oscar Wilde, who had known her as a correspondent and much admired her. Wilde, in some ways as great a critic as he was a playwright, always applied to the art of literature an unwaveringly high standard. Mrs. Craik he considered as 'one of the finest of our women writers' and, because of its moral tone and 'simple narrative power' he was much enamoured of *John Halifax.* Indeed, this book is still a cracking good read; one does wonder what Dinah Craik, or for that matter Oscar, would have made of its fairly recent revival as a television serial.

The archetypal *Sentimental Journey* appeared from the pen of Laurence Sterne, author of *Tristram Shandy* and other whimsical writings, in 1768. In the eighteenth century the word 'sentimental' had a slightly different connotation from today's; it implied, principally, an emphasis upon such tender emotions as love, and Sterne's unstructured account of his travels in France holds plenty of encounters with ladies. Notable are his comments on the horror of meeting compatriots abroad; as he says 'an Englishman does not travel to see Englishmen'. Sentimentality in our own modern sense certainly characterises a great many books about Cornwall, from the mid-nineteenth century onwards. Those who could gush about the cliff scenery, the great depths of the larger mines, and the quaint granite relics of a distant past, failed to note the extreme poverty in rural Cornwall or the distressing physical condition of so many miners. In fact, the fore-runner of Mrs. Craik's book was Wilkie Collins's *Ramble Beyond Railways* (1851) - but then Collins, like Dinah Craik, was both a realist and a more than competent writer.

In her *Unsentimental Journey,* Mrs. Craik was accompanied by two young ladies who were her nieces. They play an important if concealed part as the audience for her stated views, and allow the text to be lightened by dialogue. The text does not need that much lightening. This is a book to read on a winter's evening, or in a deck-chair, or come to that at any point in Cornwall at any time of year. One gets to know Mrs. Craik, and to like her kindness, the emphasis upon people as individuals (she has numerous shrewd portraits, not all of them flattering) and that insistent air of the good and the beautiful that so attracted Oscar Wilde. So much for style. Content is peculiarly important. This is Cornwall in the 1880s, moving into recognisably modern guise, and again and again Dinah Craik reveals accidentally some aspect, or statement of opinion, or belief, or custom, that the historian of Cornwall would not perhaps have dated as early as this. She must be correct, of course. A real journey lies behind the narrative.

i

There is also a considerable honesty. The trip to Tintagel, not the least interesting of many interesting passages, includes an outing in a rowing boat to visit some enormous sea cavern (this is probably Fire Beacon Point). The ladies never got beyond the mouth of the cave because the girls did not like it '...and never, never, never in this world shall I again behold that wonderful, mysterious sea-cave', noted their aunt sadly. However, they were not short of direct marine encounters, notably through sea-bathing, which they did with regularity. They met artists, and tourists - both commoner by the 1880s than they had been thirty years earlier - and they met real Cornish folk, whose seemingly inherent virtues much impressed Mrs. Craik. She observed, rather oddly, 'the characteristic Cornish face, not unlike the Norman type' - though it is nice to read further that she thought it 'decidedly superior to that of the inland counties of England'. King Arthur figures much, but as a literary trope and not as an article of belief. All in all, had one to review this book in 1988, the verdict would be that it is well worth publishing; and one hundred and four years after Macmillan's took that view, it is eminently worth re-publishing for the contemporary reader.

Mrs. Craik was fortunate in her illustrator. Much of the charm of *An Unsentimental Journey* resides in the thirty-five plates. Charles Napier Hemy was a Newcastle man, born in that city on 24 May 1841. He and his brothers Bernard Benedict and Thomas Marie Modawaska were pupils of W. Bell Scott's, at the Newcastle School of Art. Between 1850 and 1852 the family went to Australia and back; as a boy, C. N. Hemy worked on a brig for a time and then, deciding to enter the priesthood, spent three years in a Dominican house at Newcastle. His superiors sent him to France, to another fraternity at Lyon, but when he reached 21, Hemy resolved to give up the religious life and to become an artist full-time. As early as 1865, he exhibited at the Royal Academy, and two years later went to Antwerp to work with Baron Henri Leys, before returning to London about 1870.

C.N. Hemy at this period was producing views of the Thames, and of historical subjects, but a longstanding interest in marine art came to the fore. Soon after 1880, he moved to Falmouth - where his home was Churchfield, in Kimberley Place - and bought a yacht, the better to pursue the large oils for which he became well known. Hemy was a prolific painter; he was elected a Royal Academician in 1910 (having become an Associate in 1898), and was made R.W.S. in 1897. He painted almost to the end of his life; an enormous oil painting, a naval warfare set-piece owned by the Royal Institution of Cornwall, Truro, is dated 1915. He died at Falmouth two years later. Works by Hemy do emerge from time to time, and he is occasionally, but wrongly, linked to the Newlyn School. Very much a Falmouth artist, he must nevertheless have travelled around west Cornwall to provide Mrs. Craik with her appropriate views.

There is no clue as to why he was chosen, or whether author and artist ever met; presumably Hemy was commissioned by Macmillans, the publishers. Some of the larger plates may be based on oils, or big watercolours, and have been re-drawn on copper or zinc by engravers whose names (Paterson, Gascoin, etc.) are appended; smaller illustrations seem to be Hemy's own direct sketches. Entirely redolent of the 1880s, they are a perfect complement to the text.

But enough of this introduction. Let Dinah Maria Mulock Craik speak for herself, and let the reader decide whether or not sentimentality enters into her narrative. In the long parade of visits to Cornwall, and their all too frequent literary aftermaths, Mrs. Craik's book must still stand firmly within the half-dozen best. Its re-appearance is overdue, and as for Mrs. Craik, one can but echo the general remark of her friends, contemporaries and literary colleagues. She shines out as a very nice person. It must have been most pleasant to know Mrs. Craik, and we can meet her, retrospectively, through her writings.

Charles Thomas, Lambessow, 1988

An
Unsentimental Journey
through
Cornwall

BY
THE AUTHOR OF " JOHN HALIFAX, GENTLEMAN "

WITH ILLUSTRATIONS
BY
C. NAPIER HEMY

London
MACMILLAN AND CO.
1884

CONTENTS

LIST OF ILLUSTRATIONS

b

FALMOUTH, FROM FLUSHING.

DAY THE FIRST

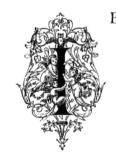

BELIEVE in holidays. Not in a frantic rushing about from place to place, glancing at everything and observing nothing; flying from town to town, from hotel to hotel, eager to "do" and to see a country, in order that when they get home they may say they have done it, and seen it. Only to say;—as for any real vision of eye, heart, and brain, they might as well go through the world blindfold. It is not the things we see, but the mind we see them with, which makes the real interest of travelling. "Eyes and No Eyes,"—an old-fashioned story about two little children taking a walk; one seeing everything, and enjoying everything, and the other seeing nothing, and thinking the expedition the dullest imaginable. This simple tale, which the present generation has probably never read, contains the essence of all rational travelling.

So when, as the "old hen," (which I am sometimes called, from my habit

B

of going about with a brood of " chickens," my own or other people's) I planned a brief tour with two of them, one just entered upon her teens, the other in her twenties, I premised that it must be a tour after my own heart.

"In the first place, my children, you must obey orders implicitly. I shall collect opinions, and do my best to please everybody ; but in travelling one only must decide, the others coincide. It will save them a world of trouble, and their 'conductor' also; who, if competent to be trusted at all, should be trusted absolutely. Secondly, take as little luggage as possible. No sensible people travel with their point-lace and diamonds. Two 'changes of raiment,' good, useful dresses, prudent boots, shawls, and waterproofs—these I shall insist upon, and nothing more. Nothing for show, as I shall take you to no place where you can show off. We will avoid all huge hotels, all fashionable towns; we will study life in its simplicity, and make ourselves happy in our own humble, feminine way. Not 'roughing it' in any needless or reckless fashion—the 'old hen' is too old for that ; yet doing everything with reasonable economy. Above all, rushing into no foolhardy exploits, and taking every precaution to keep well and strong, so as to enjoy the journey from beginning to end, and hinder no one else from enjoying it. There are four things which travellers ought never to lose : their luggage, their temper, their health, and their spirits. I will make you as happy as I possibly can, but you must also make me happy by following my rules : especially the one golden rule, Obey orders."

So preached the " old hen," with a vague fear that her chickens might turn out to be ducklings, which would be a little awkward in the region whither she proposed to take them. For if there is one place more risky than another for adventurous young people with a talent for " perpetuating themselves down prejudices," as Mrs. Malaprop would say, it is that grandest, wildest, most dangerous coast, the coast of Cornwall.

I had always wished to investigate Cornwall. This desire had existed ever since, at five years old, I made acquaintance with Jack the Giantkiller, and afterwards, at fifteen or so, fell in love with my life's one hero, King Arthur.

Between these two illustrious Cornishmen,—equally mythical, practical folk would say—there exists more similarity than at first appears. The aim of both was to uphold right and to redress wrong. Patience, self-denial ; tenderness to the weak and helpless, dauntless courage against the wicked and the strong : these, the essential elements of true manliness, characterise both the humble Jack and the kingly Arthur. And the qualities seem to have descended to more modern times. The well-known ballad :—

> "And shall they scorn Tre, Pol, and Pen ?
> And shall Trelawny die ?
> There's twenty thousand Cornishmen
> Will know the reason why,"

has a ring of the same tone, indicating the love of justice, the spirit of fidelity and bravery, as well as of that common sense which is at the root of all useful valour.

I wanted to see if the same spirit lingered yet, as I had heard it did among Cornish folk, which, it was said, were a race by themselves, honest, simple, shrewd, and kind. Also, I wished to see the Cornish land, and especially the Land's End, which I had many a time beheld in fancy, for it was a favourite landscape-dream of my rather imaginative childhood, recurring again and again, till I could almost have painted it from memory. And as year after year every chance of seeing it in its reality seemed to melt away, the desire grew into an actual craving.

After waiting patiently for nearly half a century, I said to myself, " I will conquer Fate ; I *will* go and see the Land's End."

And it was there that, after making a circuit round the coast, I proposed finally to take my " chickens."

We concocted a plan, definite yet movable, as all travelling plans should be, clear in its dates, its outline, and intentions, but subject to modifications, according to the exigency of the times and circumstances. And with that prudent persistency, without which all travelling is a mere muddle, all discomfort, disappointment, and distaste—for on whatever terms you may be with your travelling companions when you start, you are quite sure either to love them or hate them when you get home—we succeeded in carrying it out.

The 1st of September, 1881, and one of the loveliest of September days, was the day we started from Exeter, where we had agreed to meet and stay the night. There, the previous afternoon, we had whiled away an hour in the dim cathedral, and watched, not without anxiety, the flood of evening sunshine which poured through the great west window, lighting the tombs, old and new, from the Crusader, cross-legged and broken-nosed, to the white marble bas-relief which tells the story of a not less noble Knight of the Cross, Bishop Patteson. Then we wandered round the quaint old town, in such a lovely twilight, such a starry night! But—will it be a fine day to-morrow? We could but live in hope: and hope did not deceive us.

To start on a journey in sunshine feels like beginning life well. Clouds may come—are sure to come: I think no one past earliest youth goes forth into a strange region without a feeling akin to Saint Paul's "not knowing what things may befall me there." But it is always best for each to keep to himself all the shadows, and give his companions the brightness, especially if they be young companions.

And very bright were the eyes that watched the swift-moving landscape on either side of the railway: the estuary of Exe; Dawlish, with its various colouring of rock and cliff, and its pretty little sea-side houses, where family groups stood photographing themselves on our vision, as the train rushed unceremoniously between the beach and their parlour windows; then Plymouth and Saltash, where the magnificent bridge reminded us of the one over the Tay, which we had once crossed, not long before that Sunday night when, sitting in a quiet sick-room in Edinburgh, we heard the howl outside of the fearful blast which destroyed such a wonderful work of engineering art, and whirled so many human beings into eternity.

But this Saltash bridge, spanning placidly a smiling country, how pretty and safe it looked! There was a general turning to carriage-windows, and then a courteous drawing back, that we, the strangers, should see it, which broke the ice with our fellow-travellers. To whom we soon began to talk, as is our conscientious custom when we see no tangible objection thereto, and gained, now, as many a time before, much pleasant as well as useful information. Every one evinced an eager politeness to show us the country, and an innocent anxiety that we should admire it; which we could honestly do.

I shall long remember, as a dream of sunshiny beauty and peace, this journey between Plymouth and Falmouth, passing Liskeard, Lostwithiel, St. Austell, &c. The green-wooded valleys, the rounded hills, on one of which we were shown the remains of the old castle of Ristormel, noted among the three castles of Cornwall; all this, familiar to so many, was to us absolutely new, and we enjoyed it and the kindly interest that was taken in pointing it out to us, as happy-minded simple folk do always enjoy the sight of a new country.

Our pleasure seemed to amuse an old gentleman who sat in the corner. He at last addressed us, with an unctuous west-country accent which suited well his comfortable stoutness. He might have fed all his life

ST. MAWE'S CASTLE, FALMOUTH BAY.

upon Dorset butter and Devonshire cream, to one of which counties he certainly belonged. Not, I think, to the one we were now passing through, and admiring so heartily.

"So you're going to travel in Cornwall. Well, take care, they're sharp folk, the Cornish folk. They'll take you in if they can." (Then, he must be a Devon man. It is so easy to sit in judgment upon next-door neighbours.) "I don't mean to say they'll actually cheat you, but they'll take you in, and they'll be careful that you don't take them in—no, not to the extent of a brass farthing."

We explained, smiling, that we had not the slightest intention of taking anybody in, that we liked justice, and blamed no man, Cornishman or otherwise, for trying to do the best he could for himself, so that it was not to the injury of other people.

"Well, well, perhaps you're right. But they are sharp, for all that, especially in the towns."

We replied that we meant to escape towns, whenever possible, and encamp in some quiet places, quite out of the world.

Our friend opened his eyes, evidently thinking this a most singular taste.

"Well, if you really want a quiet place, I can tell you of one, almost as quiet as your grave. I ought to know, for I lived there sixteen years." (At any rate, it seemed to have agreed with him.) "Gerrans is its name— a fishing village. You get there from Falmouth by boat. The fare is "— (I regret to say my memory is not so accurate as his in the matter of pennies), "and mind you don't pay one farthing more. Then you have to drive across country; the distance is—and the fare per mile—" (Alas! again I have totally forgotten.) "They'll be sure to ask you double the money, but never you mind! refuse to pay it, and they'll give in. You must always hold your own against extortion in Cornwall."

I thanked him, with a slightly troubled mind. But I have always noticed that in travelling "with such measure as ye mete it shall be meted to you again," and that those who come to a country expecting to be cheated generally are cheated. Having still a lingering belief in human nature, and especially in Cornish nature, I determined to set down the old gentleman's well-meant advice for what it was worth, no more, and cease to perplex myself about it. For which resolve I have since been exceedingly thankful.

He gave us, however, much supplementary advice which was rather useful, and parted from us in the friendliest fashion, with that air of bland complaisance natural to those who assume the character of adviser in general.

"Mind you go to Gerrans. They'll not take you in more than they do everywhere else, and you'll find it a healthy place, and a quiet place—as quiet, I say, as your grave. It will make you feel exactly as if you were dead and buried."

That not being the prominent object of our tour in Cornwall, we thanked him again, but as soon as he left the carriage determined among ourselves to take no further steps about visiting Gerrans.

VIEW OF FLUSHING FROM THE GREEN BANK HOTEL, FALMOUTH.

However, in spite of the urgency of another fellow-traveller—it is always good to hear everybody's advice, and follow your own—we carried our love of quietness so far that we eschewed the magnificent new Falmouth Hotel, with its *table d'hôte*, lawn tennis ground, sea baths and promenade, for the old-fashioned Green Bank, which though it had no green banks, boasted, we had been told, a pleasant little sea view and bay view, and was a resting-place full of comfort and homely peace.

Which we found true, and would have liked to stay longer in its pleasant shelter, which almost conquered our horror of hotels; but we had now fairly weighed anchor and must sail on.

"You ought to go at once to the Lizard," said the friend who met us, and did everything for us at Falmouth—and the remembrance of whom, and of all that happened in our brief stay, will make the very name of the place sound sweet in our ears for ever. "The Lizard is the real point for sightseers, almost better than the Land's End. Let us see if we can hear of lodgings."

She made inquiries, and within half an hour we did hear of some most satisfactory ones. "The very thing! We will telegraph at once—answer paid," said this good genius of practicality, as sitting in her carriage she herself wrote the telegram and despatched it. Telegrams to the Lizard! We were not then at the Ultima Thule of civilisation.

"Still," she said, "you had better provide yourself with some food, such as groceries and hams. You can't always get what you want at the Lizard."

So, having the very dimmest idea what the Lizard was—whether a town, a village, or a bare rock—when we had secured the desired lodgings ("quite ideal lodgings," remarked our guardian angel), I proceeded to lay in a store of provisions, doing it as carefully as if fitting out a ship for the North Pole—and afterwards found out it was a work of supererogation entirely.

The next thing to secure was an "ideal" carriage, horse, and man, which our good genius also succeeded in providing. And now, our minds being at rest, we were able to write home a fixed address for a week, and assure our expectant and anxious friends that all was going well with us.

Then, after a twilight wander round the quaint old town—so like a foreign town—and other keen enjoyments, which, as belonging to the sanctity of private life I here perforce omit, we laid us down to sleep, and slept in peace, having really achieved much; considering it was only the first day of our journey.

DAY THE SECOND

IS there anything more delightful than to start on a smiling morning in a comfortable carriage, with all one's *impedimenta* (happily not much!) safely stowed away under one's eyes, with a good horse, over which one's feelings of humanity need not be always agonising, and a man to drive, whom one can trust to have as much sense as the brute, especially in the matter of "refreshment." Our letters that morning had brought us a comico-tragic story of a family we knew, who, migrating with a lot of children and luggage, and requiring to catch a train thirteen miles off, had engaged a driver who "refreshed himself" so successfully at every public-house on the way, that he took five hours to accomplish the journey, and finally had to be left at the road-side, and the luggage transferred to another vehicle, which of course lost the train. We congratulated ourselves that no such disaster was likely to happen to us.

"Yes; I've been a teetotaller all my life," said our driver, a bright-looking, intelligent young fellow, whom, as he became rather a prominent adjunct to our life and decidedly to our comfort, I shall individualise by calling him Charles. "I had good need to avoid drinking. My father drank through a small property. No fear of me, ma'am."

So at once between him and us, or him and "we," according to the Cornish habit of transposing pronouns, was established a feeling of fraternity, which, during the six days that we had to do with him, deepened into real regard. Never failing when wanted, never presuming when not wanted, straightforward, independent, yet full of that respectful kindliness which servants can always show and masters should always appreciate, giving us

C

a chivalrous care, which, being "unprotected females," was to us extremely valuable, I here record that much of the pleasure of our tour was owing to this honest Cornishman, who served us, his horse, and his master—he was one of the employés of a livery-stable keeper—with equal fidelity.

Certainly, numerous as were the parties he had driven—("I go to the Lizard about three times a week," he said)—Charles could seldom have driven a merrier trio than that which leisurely mounted the upland road from Falmouth, leading to the village of Constantine.

"Just turn and look behind you, ladies" (we had begged to be shown everything and told everything); "isn't that a pretty view?"

It certainly was. From the high ground we could see Falmouth with its sheltered bay and glittering sea beyond. Landward were the villages of Mabe and Constantine, with their great quarries of granite, and in the distance lay wide sweeps of undulating land, barren and treeless, but still beautiful—not with the rich pastoral beauty of our own Kent, yet having a charm of its own. And the air, so fresh and pure, yet soft and balmy, it felt to tender lungs like the difference between milk and cream. To breathe became a pleasure instead of a pain. I could quite understand how the semi-tropical plants that we had seen in a lovely garden below, grew and flourished, how the hydrangeas became huge bushes, and the eucalyptus an actual forest tree.

But this was in the sheltered valley, and we had gained the hill-top, emerging out of one of those deep-cut lanes peculiar to Devon and Cornwall, and so pretty in themselves, a perfect garden of wild flowers and ferns, except that they completely shut out the view. This did not much afflict the practical minds of my two juniors. Half an hour before they had set up a shout—

"Stop the carriage! *Do* stop the carriage! Just look there! Did you ever see such big blackberries? and what a quantity! Let us get out; we'll gather them for to-morrow's pudding."

Undoubtedly a dinner earned is the sweetest of all dinners. I remember once thinking that our cowslip tea (I should not like to drink it now) was better than our grandmother's best Bohea or something out of her lovely old tea-caddy. So the carriage, lightened of all but myself, crawled leisurely up and waited on the hill-top for the busy blackberry-gatherers.

While our horse stood cropping an extempore meal, I and his driver

A FISHERMAN'S CELLAR NEAR THE LIZARD.

began to talk about him and other cognate topics, including the permanent one of the great advantage to both body and soul in being freed all one's life long from the necessity of getting "something to drink" stronger than water.

"Yes," he said, "I find I can do as much upon tea or coffee as other men upon beer. I'm just as strong and as active, and can stand weather quite as well. It's a pretty hard life, winter and summer, driving all day,

C 2

coming in soaked, sometimes in the middle of the night, having to turn in for an hour or two, and then turn out again. And you must look after your horse, of course, before you think of yourself. Still, I stand it well, and that without a drop of beer from year's end to year's end."

I congratulated and sympathised; in return for which Charles entered heart and soul into the blackberry question, pointed out where the biggest blackberries hung, and looked indeed—he was still such a young fellow!— as if he would have liked to go blackberry-hunting himself.

I put, smiling, the careless question, "Have you any little folks of your own? Are you married?"

How cautious one should be over an idle word! All of a sudden the cheerful face clouded, the mouth began to quiver, with difficulty I saw he kept back the tears. It was a version in every-day life of Longfellow's most pathetic little poem, "The Two Locks of Hair."

"My wife broke her heart after the baby, I think. It died. She went off in consumption. It's fifteen months now"—(he had evidently counted them)—"fifteen months since I have been alone. I didn't like to give up my home and my bits of things; still, when a man has to come in wet and tired to an empty house——"

He turned suddenly away and busied himself over his horse, for just that minute the two girls came running back, laughing heartily, and showing their baskets full of "the very biggest blackberries you ever saw!"

I took them back into the carriage; the driver mounted his box, and drove on for some miles in total silence. As, when I had whispered that little episode to my two companions, so did we.

There are two ways of going from Falmouth to the Lizard—the regular route through the town of Helstone, and another, a trifle longer, through the woods of Trelowarren, the seat of the old Cornish family of Vyvyan.

"I'll take you that road, ma'am, it's much the prettiest," said Charles evidently exerting himself to recover his cheerful looks and be the civil driver and guide, showing off all the curiosities and beauties of the neighbourhood. And very pretty Trelowarren was, though nothing remarkable to us who came from the garden of England. Still, the trees were big— for Cornwall, and in the ferny glade grew abundantly the *Osmunda regalis*, a root of which we greatly coveted, and Charles offered to get. He seemed to take a pride in showing us everything, except what he probably did not know of, and which, when I heard of too late, was to me a real regret.

At Trelowarren, not far from the house, are a series of subterranean chambers and galleries, in all ninety feet long and about the height of a man. The entrance is very low. Still it is possible to get into them and traverse them from end to end, the walls being made of blocks of unhewn stone, leaning inward towards the roof, which is formed of horizontal blocks. How, when, and for what purpose this mysterious underground dwelling was made, is utterly lost in the mists of time. I should exceedingly have liked to examine it, and to think we passed close by and never knew of it will always be a certain regret, of which I relieve my mind by telling it for the guidance of other archæological travellers.

One of the charms of Cornwall is that it gives one the sense of being such an old country, as if things had gone exactly as they do now, not merely since the days of King Arthur, but for ever so long before then. The Romans, the Phœnicians, nay, the heroes of pre-historic ages, such as Jack the Giantkiller and the giant Cormoran, seemed to be not impossible myths, as we gradually quitted civilisation in the shape of a village or two, and a few isolated farm-houses, and came out upon the wild district known as Goonhilly Down.

Certainly not from its hills, for it is as flat as the back of your hand, and as bare. But the word, which is old Cornish—that now extinct tongue, which only survives in the names of places and people—means a *hunting ground;* and there is every reason to believe that this wide treeless waste was once an enormous forest, full of wild beasts. There St. Rumon, an Irish bishop, long before there were any Saxon bishops or saints, is said to have settled, far away from the world, and made a cell and oratory, the memory of which, and of himself, is still kept up by the name of the two villages, Ruan Major and Ruan Minor, on the outskirts of this Goonhilly Down.

In later times the down was noted for a breed of small, strong ponies, called "Goonhillies." Charles had heard of them, but I do not suppose he had ever heard of St. Rumon, or of the primeval forest. At present, the fauna of Goonhilly is represented by no animal more dangerous than a rabbit or a field-mouse, and its vegetation includes nothing bigger than the *erica vagans*—the lovely Cornish heath, lilac, flesh-coloured and white which will grow nowhere else, except in a certain district of Portugal.

"There it is!" we cried, at the pleasant first sight of a new flower: for though not scientific botanists, we have what I may call a speaking acquaintance with almost every wild flower that grows. To see one that we had never seen before was quite an excitement. Instantly we were out of the carriage, and gathering it by handfuls.

Botanists know this heath well—it has the peculiarity of the anthers being outside instead of inside the bell—but we only noticed the beauty of it, the masses in which it grew, and how it would grow only within a particular line—the sharp geological line of magnesian earth, which forms the serpentine district. Already we saw, forcing itself up through the turf, blocks of this curious stone, and noticed how cottage-walls were built, and fences made of it.

"Yes, that's the serpentine," said Charles, now in his depth once more; we could not have expected him to know about St. Rumon, &c. "You'll see plenty of it when you get to the Lizard. All the coast for miles and miles is serpentine. Such curious rocks, reddish and greenish; they look so pretty when the water washes against them, and when polished, and made into ornaments, candlesticks, brooches and the like. But I'll show you the shops as we pass. We shall be at Lizard Town directly."

So it was a town, and it had shops. We should not have thought so, judging by the slender line of white dots which now was appearing on the horizon—Cornish folk seemed to have a perfect mania for painting their houses a glistening white. Yes, that was the Lizard; we were nearing our journey's end. At which we were a little sorry, even though already an hour or two behind-hand—that is, behind the hour we had ordered dinner. But "time was made for slaves"—and railway travellers, and we were beyond railways.

"Never mind, what does dinner matter?" (It did not seriously, as we had taken the precaution, which I recommend to all travellers, of never starting on any expedition without a good piece of bread, a bunch of raisins, and a flask of cold tea or coffee.) "What's the odds so long as you're happy? Let us linger and make the drive as long as we can. The horse will not object, nor Charles either."

Evidently not; our faithful steed cropped contentedly an extempore meal, and Charles, who would have scrambled anywhere or dug up anything "to please the young ladies," took out his pocket-knife, and devoted himself to the collection of all the different coloured heaths; roots which we determined to send home in the hope, alas! I fear vain, that they would grow in our garden,. afar from their native magnesia.

So for another peaceful hour we stayed; wandering about upon Goonhilly Down. How little it takes to make one happy, when one wants to be happy, and knows enough of the inevitable sorrows of life to be

THE CORNISH COAST: FROM YNYS HEAD TO BEAST POINT.

glad to be happy—as long as fate allows. Each has his burthen to bear, seen or unseen by the world outside, and some of us that day had not a light one; yet was it a bright day, a white day, a day to be thankful for.

Nor did it end when, arriving at the "ideal" lodgings, and being received with a placidity which we felt we had not quite deserved, and fed in a manner which reflected much credit not only on the cook's skill, but her temper—we sallied out to see the place.

Not a picturesque place exactly. A high plain, with the sparkling sea beyond it; the principal object near being the Lizard Lights, a huge low building, with a tower at either side, not unlike the Sydenham Crystal palace, only dazzling white, as every building apparently was at the Lizard.

"We'll go out and adventure," cried the young folks; and off they started down the garden, over a stile—made of serpentine of course—and across what seemed a field, till they disappeared mysteriously where the line of sea cut the line of cliffs, and were heard of no more for two hours.

Then they returned, all delight and excitement. They had found such a lovely little cove, full of tiny pools, a perfect treasure-house of sea-weeds and sea-anemones; and the rocks, so picturesque, and "so grand to scramble over." (I must confess that to these, my practically-minded "chickens," the picturesque or the romantic always ranked second to the fun of a scramble.) The descent to this marine paradise also seemed difficult enough to charm anybody.

"But *you* wouldn't do it. Quite impossible! You would break all your legs and arms, and sprain both your ankles."

Alas, for a hen—and an old hen—with ducklings! But mine, though daring, were not rash, and had none of that silly fool-hardiness which for the childish vanity of doing, or of saying one has done, a dangerous thing, risks health, comfort, life, and delights selfishly in making other people utterly miserable. So, being feeble on my feet, though steady in my head, I agreed to sit like a cormorant on the nearest cliff, and look down placidly upon the young adventurers in their next delightful scramble.

It could not be to-night, however, for the tide was coming in fast; the fairy cove would soon be all under water.

"Shall we get a boat? It will soon be sunset and moon-rise; we can watch both from the sea."

That sea! Its broad circle had no other bound than the shores of America, and its blueness, or the strange, changing tint often called blue, almost equalled the blue of the Mediterranean.

"Yes, ma'am, it's a fine evening for a row," said the faithful Charles. "And it isn't often you can get a row here; the sea is so rough, and the landing so difficult. But there's a man I know; he has a good boat, he knows the coast well, and he'll not go out unless it's really safe."

This seemed ultra-prudent, with such a smiling sky and sea; but we soon found it was not unnecessary at the Lizard. Indeed all along the Cornish coast the great Atlantic waves come in with such a roll or a heavy ground-swell, windless, but the precursor of a storm that is slowly arriving from across the ocean, that boating here at best is no child's play.

We had been fair-weather sailors, over shut-in lochs or smooth rivers; all of us could handle an oar, or had handled it in old days, but this was a different style of thing. Descending the steep zigzag path to the next cove— the only one where there was anything like a fair landing—we found we still had to walk through a long bed of sea-weed, and manage somehow to get into the boat between the recoil and advance of a wave. Not one of the tiny waves of quiet bays, but an Atlantic roller, which, even if comparatively small and tame, comes in with a force that will take you off your feet at any time.

However, we managed it, and found ourselves floating among an archipelago of rocks, where the solemn cormorants sat in rows, and affectionate families of gulls kept swimming about in a large flotilla of white dots on the dark water. Very dark the sea was: heaving and sinking in great hills and valleys, which made rowing difficult. Also, for several yards round every rock extended a perfect whirlpool of foaming waves, which, if any boat chanced to be caught therein, would have dashed it to pieces in no time. But our boatmen seemed used to the danger, and took us as near it as possible, without actually running into it.

They were both far from commonplace-looking men, especially the elder, our stroke-oar. Being rather given to ethnological tastes, we had already noticed the characteristic Cornish face, not unlike the Norman type, and decidedly superior to that of the inland counties of England. But this was a face by itself, which would have attracted any artist or student of human nature; weather-beaten, sharp-lined, wrinkled as it was—the man must have been fully sixty—there was in it a sweetness, an absolute beauty, which struck us at once. The smile, placid and paternal, came often, though words were few; and the keen, kindly eyes were blue as a child's, or as Tennyson describes King Arthur's.

"I can imagine," whispered one of us who had imaginative tendencies, "that King Arthur might have looked thus, had he lived to grow old."

D

"I don't believe King Arthur ever lived at all," was the knock-me-down utilitarian answer, to which the other had grown accustomed and indifferent. Nevertheless, there was such a refinement about the man, spite of his rough fisherman's dress, and he had been so kind to the young folks, so considerate to "the old lady," as Cornish candour already called me, that, intending to employ him again, we asked his name.

"John Curgenven."

"John what?" We made several hopeless plunges at it, and finally asked him to spell it.

"Cur-gen-ven," said he; adding, with a slight air of pride, "one of the oldest families in Cornwall."

(I have no hesitation in stating this, because, when we afterwards became great friends, I told John Curgenven I should probably "put him in a book"—if he had no objection. To which he answered with his usual composure, "No, he did not think it would harm him." He evidently considered "writing a book" was a very inferior sort of trade.)

But looking at him, one could not help speculating as to how far the legend of King Arthur had been really true, and whether the type of man which Tennyson has preserved—or created—in this his "own ideal knight," did once exist, and still exists, in a modified modern form, throughout Cornwall. A fancy upon which we then only argued; now I, at least, am inclined to believe it.

"There is Lord Brougham's head, his wig and his turn-up nose, you can see all distinctly. At least, you could if there was light enough."

But there was not light, for the sun was setting, and the moon only just rising. Black looked the heaving sea, except where rings of white foam encircled each group of rocks, blacker still. And blackest of all looked the iron-bound coast, sharp against the amber western sky.

"Yes, that's Kynance Cove, and the Gull Rock and Asparagus Island. Shall we row there? It's only about two miles."

Two miles there, and two back, through this angry sea, and then to land in the dim light about 9 p.m.! Courage failed us. We did not own this; we merely remarked that we would rather see Kynance by daylight, but I think each of us felt a sensation of relief when the boat's head was turned homewards.

Yet how beautiful it all was! Many a night afterwards we watched the same scene, but never lovelier than that night, the curved line of coast traceable distinctly up to Mount's Bay, and then the long peninsula which they told us was the Land's End, stretching out into the horizon, where sea and sky met in a mist of golden light, through which the sun was slowly dropping right from the sky into the sea. Beyond was a vague cloud-land, which might be the fair land of Lyonesse itself, said still to lie there submerged, with all its cities and towers and forests; or the "island-valley of Avillion," whither Arthur sailed with the three queens to be healed of his "grievous wound," and whence he is to come again some day. Popular superstition still expects him, and declares that he haunts this coast even now in the shape of a Cornish chough.

Modern ghosts, too, exist, decidedly more alarming.

"Look up there, ladies, that green slope is Pistol Meadow. Nobody likes to walk there after dark. Other things walk as well."

"What things?"

"Two hundred and more of foreign sailors, whose ship went to pieces in the little cove below. They're buried under the green mounds you see. Out of a crew of seven hundred only two men were washed ashore alive, and they were in irons, which the captain had put on them because they said he was going too near in shore. It was called Pistol Meadow because most of 'em were found with pistols in their hands, which may have been true or may not, since it happened more than a hundred years ago. However, there are the green mounds, you see, and Lizard folk don't much like passing the place after dark."

"But you?"

John Curgenven smiled. "Oh, us and the coast-guards! Us goes anywhere, at all hours, and never meets nothing. D'ye see those white marks all along the coast every few yards? They're rocks, kept white-washed, to guide the men of dark nights between here and Kynance. It's a ticklish path, when all's as black as pitch, with a stiff wind blowing."

I should think it was! One almost shuddered at the idea, and then felt proud of the steady heads and cool courage of these coast-guard men— always the pick of the service, true Englishmen, fearless and faithful—the business of whose whole lives is to save other lives—that is, now that smuggling has abated, and those dreadful stories once current all along the

D 2

coast of Cornwall have become mostly legends of the past. No tales of wreckers, or of fights between smugglers and revenue officers, reached our ears, but the stories of shipwrecks were endless. Every winter, and many times through the winter, some ghastly tragedy had happened. Every half-mile along this picturesque shore was recorded the place where some good ship went to pieces, often with the brief addendum, "all hands lost."

"The sun's just setting. Look out for the Lizard Lights," called out Charles, who sat in the bow of the boat in faithful attendance upon his "ladies,"—another Knight of the Round Table in humble life—we met many such in Cornwall. "Look! There they are."

And sure enough, the instant the sun's last spark was quenched in the sea, into which he dropped like a red round ball, out burst two substitute suns, and very fair substitutes too, making the poor little moon in the east of no importance whatever. The gleam of them extended far out upon the darkening ocean, and we could easily believe that their light was "equal to 20,000 candles," and that they were seen out at sea to a distance of twenty, some said even thirty, miles.

"Except in a fog; and the fogs at the Lizard are very bad. Then you can see nothing, not even the Lights, but they keep sounding the fog-horn every minute or so. It works by the same machinery as works the Lights—a big steam-engine; you can hear it bum-bumming now, if you listen."

So we could, a mysterious noise like that of a gigantic bumble-bee, coming across the water from that curious building, long and white, with its two towers and those great eyes in each of them, at either end.

"They're wonderful bright;" said John Curgenven; "many's the time I've sat and read my newspaper by them a quarter of a mile off. They're seen through the blackest night, the blacker the brighter, seen through everything—except fog. Now, ladies, d'ye think you can jump ashore?"

Some of us did, airily enough, though it required to choose your moment pretty cleverly so as to escape the incoming wave. And some of us—well, we accepted the inevitable, and were only too thankful to scramble anyhow, wet or dry, on terra firma.

And then we had to ascend the zigzag path, slippery with loose stones, and uncertainly seen in the dim half-twilight, half-moonlight. At last we came out safe by the life-boat house, which we had noticed in passing, with

THE LIZARD LIGHTS BY NIGHT.

the slit in its door for "Contributions," and a notice below that the key was kept at such and such a house—I forget the man's name—"and at the Rectory."

"Yes," said Curgenven, "in many places along this coast, when there's a wreck, and we're called out, the parson's generally at the head of us. Volunteers? Of course we're all volunteers, except the coast-guard, who are paid. But they're often glad enough of us and of our boats too. The life-boat isn't enough. They keep her here, the only place they can, but it's tough work running her down to the beach on a black winter's night, with a ship going to pieces before your eyes, as ships do here in no time. I've seen it myself—watched her strike, and in ten minutes there was not a bit of her left."

We could well imagine it. Even on this calm evening the waves kept dashing themselves against every rock with a roar and a swell and a circle of boiling foam. What must it be on a stormy winter night, or through the deathly quiet of a white mist, with nothing visible or audible except the roar of the waters and the shriek of the fog-horn!

"I think it's full time we were in-doors," suggested a practical and prudent little voice; "we can come again and see it in the daylight. Here's the road."

"That's the way you came, Miss," said Charles, "but I can take you a much shorter one on the top of the hedges"—or edges, we never quite knew which they were, though on the whole the letter *h* is tolerably well treated in Cornwall.

These "hedges" were startling to any one not Cornish-born. In the Lizard district the divisions of land are made not by fences, but by walls, built in a peculiar fashion, half stones, half earth, varying from six to ten feet high, and about two feet broad. On the top of this narrow giddy path, fringed on either side by deceitful grass, you are expected to walk!—in fact, are obliged to walk, for there is often no other road. There was none here.

I looked round in despair. Once upon a time I could have walked upon walls as well as anybody, but now—!

"I'll help you, ma'am; and I'm sure you can manage it," said Charles consolingly. "It's only three-quarters of a mile."

Three-quarters of a mile along a two-foot path on the top of a wall, and in this deceitful light, when one false step would entail a certain fall. And at my age one doesn't fall exactly like a feather or an india-rubber ball.

"Ma'am, if you go slow and steady, with me before and Curgenven behind, you'll *not* fall."

Nor did I. I record it with gratitude to those two honest men—true *gentlemen*, such as I have found at times in all ranks—who never once grumbled or relaxed in their care of their tardy and troublesome charge; one instance more of that kindly courtesy which it does any man good to offer, and which any woman, "lady" though she be, may feel proud to receive.

When we reached "home," as we had already begun to call it, a smiling face and a comfortable tea justified the word. And when we retired, a good deal fatigued, but quite happy, we looked out upon the night, where the fiery stream of the Lizard Lights was contending with the brightest of harvest moons. It was a hopeful ending of our second day.

CORNISH FISH.

DAY THE THIRD

"AND a beautiful day it is, ladies, though it won't do for Kynance."

Only 8 a.m., yet there stood the faithful Charles, hat in hand, having heard that his ladies were at breakfast, and being evidently anxious that they should not lose an hour of him and his carriage, which were both due at Falmouth to-night. For this day was Saturday, and we were sending him home for Sunday.

"As I found out last night, the tide won't suit for Kynance till Wednesday or Thursday, and you'll be too tired to walk much to-day. I've been thinking it all over. Suppose I were to drive you to Kennack Sands, back by the serpentine works to Cadgwith, and home to dinner? Then after dinner I'll give the horse a rest for two hours, and take you to Mullion; we can order tea at Mary Mundy's, and go on to the cove as far as I can get with the carriage. I'll leave it at the farm and be in time to help you over the rocks to see the caves, run ahead and meet you again with the carriage, and drive you back to Mary Mundy's. You can have tea and be home in the moonlight before nine o'clock."

"And you?" we asked, a good deal bewildered by this carefully-outlined plan and all the strange names of places and people, yet not a little touched by the kindly way in which we were "taken in and done for" by our faithful squire of dames.

"Me, ma'am? Oh, after an hour or two's rest the horse can start again —say at midnight, and be home by daylight. Or we could go to bed and be up early at four, and still get to Falmouth by eight, in time for the church work. Don't you trouble about us, we'll manage. He" (the other

E

and four-footed half of the "we") "is a capital animal, and he'd get much harder work than this if he was at home."

So we decided to put ourselves entirely in the hands of Charles, who seemed to have our interest so much at heart, and yet evinced a tenderness over his horse that is not too common among hired drivers. We promised to be ready in half an hour, so as to waste nothing of this lovely day, in which we had determined to enjoy ourselves.

Who could help it? It was delightful to wake up early and refreshed, and come down to this sunshiny, cheerful breakfast-table, where, though nothing was grand, all was thoroughly comfortable.

"I'm sure you're very kind, ladies, to be so pleased with everything," apologised our bright-looking handmaiden; "and since you really wish to keep this room"—a very homely parlour which we had chosen in preference to a larger one, because it looked on the sea—"I only wish things was better for you; still, if you can make shift—"

Well, if travellers cannot "make shift" with perfectly clean tidy rooms, well-cooked plain food, and more than civil, actually kindly, attendance, they ought to be ashamed of themselves! So we declared we would settle down in the evidently despised little parlour.

It was not an æsthetic apartment, certainly. The wall-paper and carpet would have driven Morris and Co. nearly frantic; the furniture—mere chairs and a table—belonged "to the year one"—but (better than many modern chairs and tables) you could sit down upon the first and dine upon the second, in safety. There was no sofa, so we gladly accepted an offered easy-chair, and felt that all really useful things were now ours.

But the ornamental? There was a paper arrangement in the grate, and certain vases on the chimney-piece which literally made our hair stand on end! After a private consultation as to how far we might venture, without wounding the feelings of our landlady, we mildly suggested that "perhaps we could do without these ornaments." All we wanted in their stead were a few jars, salt-jars or jam-pots, in which to arrange our wild flowers, of which yesterday the girls had gathered a quantity.

The exchange was accepted, though with some surprise. But when, half an hour afterwards, the parlour appeared quite transformed, decorated in every available corner with brilliant autumn flowers—principally yellow—intermixed with the lovely Cornish heath; when, on some excuse or other, the hideous "ornament for your fire-stoves" was abolished, and the grate filled with a mass of green fern and grey sea-holly—I know no combination more exquisite both as to colour and form—then we felt that we could survive, at least for a week, even if shut up within this humble room, innocent of the smallest attraction as regarded art, music, or literature.

But without doors? There Nature beat Art decidedly.

What a world it was! Literally swimming in sunshine, from the sparkling sea in the distance, to the beds of marigolds close by—huge marigolds, double and single, mingled with carnations that filled the air with rich autumnal scent, all the more delicious because we feel it is autumnal, and therefore cannot last. It was a very simple garden, merely a square grass-plot with a walk and a border round it, and its only flowers were these marigolds, carnations, with quantities of mignonette, and bounded all round with a hedge of tamarisk; yet I think we shall always remember it as if it were the Garden of Armida—without a Tancred to spoil it!

For—under the rose—one of the pleasures of our tour was that it was so exclusively feminine. We could feed as we liked, dress as we liked, talk to whom we liked, without any restriction, from the universal masculine sense of dignity and decorum in travelling. We felt ourselves unconventional, incognito, able to do exactly as we chose, provided we did nothing wrong.

So off we drove through Lizard Town into the "wide, wide world;" and I repeat, what a world it was! Full filled with sunlight, and with an atmosphere so fresh and bracing, yet so dry and mild and balmy, that every breath was a pleasure to draw. We had felt nothing like it since we stood on the top of the highest peak in the Island of Capri, looking down on the blue Mediterranean. But this sea was equally blue, the sky equally clear, yet it was home—dear old England, so often misprized. Yet, I believe, when one does get really fine English weather, there is nothing like it in the whole world.

The region we traversed was not picturesque—neither mountains, nor glens, nor rivers, nor woods; all was level and bare, for the road lay mostly inland, until we came out upon Kennack Sands.

They might have been the very "yellow sands" where Shakespeare's elves were bidden to "take hands" and "foot it featly here and there."

E 2

You might almost have searched for the sea-maids' footsteps along the smooth surface where the long Atlantic waves crept harmlessly in, making a glittering curve, and falling with a gentle "thud"—the only sound in the solitary bay, until all at once we caught voices and laughter, and from among some rock, emerged a party of girls.

They had evidently come in a cart, which took up its station beside our carriage, laden with bundles which looked uncommonly like bathing gowns; and were now seeking a convenient dressing-room—one of those rock-parlours, roofed with serpentine and floored with silver sand—which are the sole bathing establishments here.

All along the Cornish coast the bathing is delightful—when you can get it; but sometimes for miles and miles the cliffs rise in a huge impregnable wall, without a single break. Then perhaps there comes a sudden cleft in the rock, a green descent, possibly with a rivulet trickling through it, and leading to a sheltered cove or a sea-cave, accessible only at low water, but one of the most delicious little nooks that could be imagined. Kynance, we were told, with its "kitchen" and "drawing-room," was the most perfect specimen of the kind; but Kennack was sufficiently lovely. With all sorts of fun, shouting, and laughter, the girls disappeared to their evidently familiar haunts, to reappear as merry mermaids playing about in a crystalline sea.

A most tantalising sight to my two, who vowed never again to attempt a day's excursion without taking bathing dresses, towels, and the inevitable fish-line, to be tied round the waist,—with a mother holding the other end. For we had been warned against these long and strong Atlantic waves, the recoil of which takes you off your feet even in calm weather. As bathing must generally be done at low water, to ensure a sandy floor and a comfortable cave, it is easy enough to be swept out of one's depth; and the cleverest swimmer, if tossed about among these innumerable rocks circled round by eddies of boiling white water, would have small chance of returning with whole bones, or of returning at all.

Indeed, along this Cornish coast, life and death seem very near together. Every pleasure carries with it a certain amount of risk; the utmost caution is required both on land and sea, and I cannot advise either rash or nervous people to go travelling in Cornwall.

Bathing being impracticable, we consoled ourselves with ascending the sandy hillock, which bounded one side of the bay, and sat looking from it towards the coast-line eastwards.

POLTESCO.

What a strange peace there is in a solitary shore, an empty sea, for the one or two white dots of silent ships seemed rather to add to than diminish its loneliness—lonelier in sunshine, I think, than even in storm. The latter gives a sense of human life, of struggle and of pain ; while the former is all repose, the bright but solemn repose of infinity or eternity.

But these thoughts were for older heads ; the only idea of the young heads—uncommonly steady they must have been !—was of scrambling into the most inaccessible places, and getting as near to the sea as possible without actually tumbling into it. After a while the land attracted them in turn, and they came back with their hands full of flowers, some known, some unknown ; great bunches of honeysuckle, curious sand-plants, and cliff-plants ; also water-plants, which fringed a little rivulet that ran into the bay, while, growing everywhere abundantly, was the lovely grey-green cringo, or sea-holly.

All these treasures, to make the parlour pretty, required much ingenuity to carry home safely, the sun withered them so fast. But there was the pleasure of collecting.

We could willingly have stayed here all day—how natural is that wish of poor young Shelley, that in every pretty place he saw he might remain "for ever" !—but the forenoon was passing, and we had much to see.

"Poltesco, everybody goes to Poltesco," observed the patient Charles.

So of course we went there too. At Poltesco are the principal serpentine works—the one commerce of the district. The monotonous hum of its machinery mingled oddly with the murmur of a trout-stream which ran through the pretty little valley, crossed by a wooden bridge, where a solitary angler stood fishing in imperturbable content.

There were only about a dozen workmen visible ; one of whom came forward and explained to us the mode of work, afterwards taking us to the show-room, which contained everything possible to be made of serpentine, from mantelpieces and tombstones, down to brooches and studs. Very deli-cate and beautiful was the workmanship ; the forms of some of the things —vases and candlesticks especially—were quite Pompeian. In truth, throughout Cornwall, we often came upon shapes, Roman or Greek, proving how even yet relics of its early masters or colonisers linger in this western corner of England.

In its inhabitants too. When, as we passed, more than one busy workman lifted up his head for a moment, we noticed faces almost classic in type, quite different from the bovine, agricultural Hodge of the midland counties.

In manner different likewise. There was neither stupidity nor servility, but a sort of dignified independence. No pressing to buy, no looking out for gratuities, only a kindly politeness, which did not fail even when we departed, taking only a few little ornaments. We should have liked to carry off a cart-load—especially two enormous vases and a chimney-piece—but travellers have limits to luggage, and purse as well.

Pretty Poltesco! we left it with regret, but we were in the hands of the ever-watchful Charles, anxious that we should see as much as possible.

"The driving-road goes far inland, but there's a splendid cliff-walk from Poltesco to Cadgwith direct. The young ladies might do it with a guide—here he is, a man I know, quite reliable. They'll walk it easily in half an hour. But you, ma'am, I think you'd better come with me."

No fighting against fate. So I put my "chickens" in safe charge, meekly re-entered the carriage, and drove, humbly and alone, across a flat dull country, diversified here and there by a few cottages, politely called a village—the two villages of Ruan Minor and Ruan Major. I afterwards found that they were not without antiquarian interest, that I might have gone to examine a curious old church, well, and oratory, supposed to have been inhabited by St. Rumon. But we had left the guide-book at home, with the so longed-for bathing gowns, and Charles was not of archæological mind, so I heard nothing and investigated nothing.

Except, indeed, numerous huge hand-bills, posted on barn doors and gates, informing the inhabitants that an Exhibition of Fine Arts, admittance one shilling, was on view close by. Charles was most anxious I should stop and visit it, saying it was "very fine." But as within the last twelve-month I had seen the Royal Academy, Grosvenor Gallery, and most of the galleries and museums in Italy, the Fine Art Exhibition of Ruan Minor was not overwhelmingly attractive. However, not to wound the good Cornishman, who was evidently proud of it, I explained that, on the whole, I preferred nature to art.

And how grand nature was in this fishing-village of Cadgwith, to which after a long round, we came at last!

Nestled snugly in a bend of the coast which shelters it from north and east, leaving it open to southern sunshine, while another curve of land protects it from the dense fogs which are so common at the Lizard, Cadgwith is, summer and winter, one of the pleasantest nooks imaginable. The climate, Charles told me, is so mild, that invalids often settle down in the one inn—a mere village inn externally, but very comfortable.   And, as I

CADGWITH COVE.

afterwards heard at Lizard Town, the parson and his wife—"didn't I know them?" and I felt myself rather looked down upon because I did not know them—are the kindest of people, who take pleasure in looking after the invalids, rich or poor. "Yes," Charles considered Cadgwith was a nice place to winter in, "only just a trifle dull."

Probably so, to judge by the interest which, even in this tourist-season, our carriage excited, as we wound down one side and up another of the ravine in which the village is built, with a small fishing-station at the bottom, rather painfully odoriferous. The fisher-wives came to their doors, the old fisher-men stood, hands in pockets, the roly-poly healthy fisher-children stopped playing, to turn round and stare. In these parts everybody stares at everybody, and generally everybody speaks to every-body—a civil "good-day" at any rate, sometimes more.

"This is a heavy pull for you," said a sympathetic old woman, who had watched me leave the carriage and begin mounting the cliff towards the Devil's Frying-pan—the principal thing to be seen at Cadgwith. She followed me, and triumphantly passed me, though she had to carry a bag of potatoes on her back. I wondered if her feeling was pity or envy towards another old person who had to carry nothing but her own self. Which, alas! was enough!

She and I sat down together on the hill-side and had a chat, while I waited for the two little black dots which I could see moving round the opposite headland. She gave me all kinds of information, in the simple way peculiar to country folk, whose innocent horizon comprises the whole world, which, may be, is less pleasant than the little world of Cadgwith. Then we parted for ever and aye.

The Devil's Frying-pan is a wonderful sight. Imagine a natural amphitheatre two acres in extent, inclosed by a semi-circular slope about two hundred feet high, covered with grass and flowers and low bushes. Outside, the wide, open sea, which pours in to the shingly beach at the bottom through an arch of serpentine, the colouring of which, and of the other rocks surrounding it, is most exquisite, varying from red to green, with sometimes a tint of grey. Were Cadgwith a little nearer civilisation, what a show-place it would become!

But happily civilisation leaves it alone. The tiny farm-house on the hill-side near the Frying-pan looked, within and without, much as it must have looked for the last hundred years; and the ragged, unkempt, tongue-tied little girl, from whom we succeeded in getting a drink of milk in a

F

tumbler which she took five minutes to search for, had certainly never been to a Board School. She investigated the penny which we deposited as if

THE DEVIL'S FRYING PAN, NEAR CADGWITH.

it were a great natural curiosity rarely attainable, and she gazed after us as we climbed the stile leading to the Frying-pan as if wondering what on earth could tempt respectable people, who had nothing to do, into such a very uncomfortable place.

Uncomfortable, certainly, as we sat with our feet stuck in the long grass to prevent slipping down the slope—a misadventure which would have been, to say the least, awkward. Those boiling waves, roaring each after each through the arch below; and those jagged rocks, round which innumerable sea-birds were flying—one could quite imagine that were any luckless vessel to find itself in or near the Frying-pan, it would never get out again.

To meditative minds there is something very startling in the perpetual contrast between the summer tourist-life, so cheerful and careless, and the winter life of the people here, which must be so full of privations; for one half the year there is nothing to do, no market for serpentine, and almost no fishing possible: they have to live throughout the dark days upon the hay made while the sun shines.

"No, no," said one of the Lizard folk, whom I asked if there was much drunkenness thereabout, for I had seen absolutely none; "no, us don't drink; us can't afford it. Winter's a bad time for we—sometimes for four months a man doesn't earn a halfpenny. He has to save in summer, or he'd starve the rest of the year."

Which apparently is not altogether bad for him. I have seldom seen, in any part of England or Scotland, such an honest, independent, respectable race as the working people on this coast, and indeed throughout Cornwall.

We left with regret the pretty village, resolving to come back again in a day or two; it was barely three miles from the Lizard, though the difference in climate was said to be so great. And then we drove back across the bleak down and through the keen "hungry" sea-air, which made dinner a matter of welcome importance. And without dwelling too much on the delights of the flesh—very mild delights after all—I will say that the vegetables grown in the garden, and the grapes in the simple greenhouse beside it, were a credit to Cornwall, especially so near the sea-coast.

We had just time to dine, repose a little, and communicate our address to our affectionate friends at home—so as to link ourselves for a few brief days with the outside world—when appeared the punctual Charles.

"Don't be afraid, ladies, he's had a good rest,"—this was the important animal about whose well-being we were naturally anxious. Charles patted his shoulder, and a little person much given to deep equine affections tenderly stroked his nose. He seemed sensible of the attention and of what was expected from him, and started off, as lively as if he had been idle for a week, across the Lizard Down and Pradenack Down to Mullion.

"I hope Mary will be at home," said Charles, turning round as usual to converse; "she'll be sure to make you comfortable. Of course you've heard of Mary Mundy?"

Fortunately we had. There was in one of our guide-books a most glowing description of the Old Inn, and also an extract from a poem, apostrophising the charms of Mary Mundy. When we said we knew the enthusiastic Scotch Professor who had written it, we felt that we rose a step in the estimation of Charles.

"And Mary will be so pleased to see anybody who knows the gentleman"—in Cornwall the noted Greek Professor was merely "the gentleman." "She's got his poem in her visitors' book and his portrait in her album. I do hope Mary will be at home."

But fate was against us. When we reached Mullion and drove up to the door of the Old Inn, there darted out to meet us, not Mary, but an individual concerning whom Fame has been unjustly silent.

"It's only Mary's brother," said Charles, with an accent of deep disappointment.

But as the honest man who had apparently gone through life as "Mary's brother" stood patting our horse and talking to our driver, with both of whom he seemed on terms of equal intimacy, his welcome to ourselves was such a mixture of cordiality and despair that we could scarcely keep from laughing.

"Mary's gone to Helstone, ladies; her would have been delighted, but her's gone marketing to Helstone. I hope her'll be back soon, for I doesn't know what to do without she. The house is full, and there's a party of eleven come to tea, and actually wanting it sent down to them at the Cove. They won't get it though. And you shall get your tea, ladies, even if they have to go without."

We expressed our gratitude, and left Charles to arrange all for us, which he did in the most practical way.

"And you think Mary may be back at six?"

"Her said her would, and I hope her will," answered the brother despondently. "Her's very seldom out; us can't get on at all without she."

This, and several more long and voluble speeches given in broad Cornish, with the true Cornish confusion of pronouns, and with an air of piteous perplexity—nay, abject helplessness, the usual helplessness of man without woman—proved too much for our risible nerves. We maintained a decorous gravity till we had driven away, and then fell into shouts of laughter—the innocent laughter of happy-minded people over the smallest joke or the mildest species of fun.

"Never mind, ladies, you'll get your tea all right. If Mary said she'd be back at six, back she'll be. And you'll find a capital tea waiting for you; there isn't a more comfortable inn in all Cornwall."

Which, we afterwards found, was saying a great deal.

Mullion Cove is a good mile from Mullion village, and as we jolted over the rough road I was remorseful over both carriage and horse.

"Not at all, ma'am, he's used to it. Often and often he comes here with pic-nic parties, all the way from Falmouth. I'll put him in at the farm, and be down with you at the Cove directly. You'll find the rocks pretty bad walking, but there's a cave which you ought to see. We'll try it."

There was no resisting the way the kindly young Cornishman thus identified himself with our interests, and gave himself all sorts of extra trouble on our account. And when after a steep and not too savoury descent—the cove being used as a fish cellar—we found ourselves on the beach, shut in by those grand rocks of serpentine, with Mullion Island lying ahead about a quarter of a mile off, we felt we had not come here for nothing.

The great feature of Mullion Cove is its sea-caves, of which there are two, one on the beach, the other round the point, and only accessible at low water. Now, we saw the tide was rising fast.

"They'll have to wade; I told them they would have to wade!" cried an anxious voice behind me; and "I was ware," as ancient chroniclers say, of the presence of another "old hen," the same whom we had noticed conducting her brood of chickens, or ducklings—they seemed more like the latter now—to bathe on Kennack Sands.

"Yes, they have been away more than half an hour, all my children except this one"—a small boy who looked as if he wished he had gone too. "They would go, though I warned them they would have to wade. And there they are, just going into the cave. One, two, three, four, five, six," counting the black specks that were seen moving on, or rather in, the water. "Oh dear, they've *all* gone in! I wish they were safe out again."

Nevertheless, in the midst of her distress, the benevolent lady stopped

MULLION COVE, CORNWALL.

to give me a helping hand into the near cave, a long, dark passage, with light at either end. My girls had already safely threaded it and come triumphantly out at the other side. But what with the darkness and the uncertain footing over what felt like beds of damp seaweed, with occasional stones, through which one had to grope every inch of one's way, my heart rather misgave me, until I was cheered by the apparition of the faithful Charles.

"Don't go back, ma'am, you'll be so sorry afterwards. I'll strike a light and help you. Slow and steady, you'll come to no harm. And it's beautiful when you get out at the other end."

So it was. The most exquisite little nook; where you could have imagined a mermaid came daily to comb her hair; one can easily believe in mermaids or anything else in Cornwall. What a charming dressing-room she would have, shut in on three sides by those great walls of serpentine, and in front the glittering sea, rolling in upon a floor of the loveliest silver sand.

But the only mermaid there was an artist's wife, standing beside her husband's easel, at which he was painting away so earnestly that he scarcely noticed us. Very picturesque he looked, and she too, in her rough serge dress, with her pretty bare feet and ankles, the shoes and stockings lying in a corner as if they had not been worn for hours. Why should they be? they were quite unnecessary on those soft sands, and their owner stood and talked with me as composedly as if it were the height of the fashion to go barefoot. And far more than anything concerning herself, she seemed interested in my evident interest in the picture, which promised to be a remarkably good one, and which, if I see it on the R. A. walls next year will furnish my only clue to the identity of the couple, or theirs to mine.

But the tide was fast advancing; they began to take down the easel, and I remembered that the narrow winding cave was our only way out from this rock-inclosed fairy paradise to the prosaic beach.

"Look, they are wading ashore up to the knees! And we shall have to wade too if we don't make haste back."

So cried the perplexed mother of the six too-adventurous ducklings. But mine, more considerate, answered me from the rocks where they were scrambling, and helped me back through the cave into safe quarters, where we stood watching the waders with mingled excitement and—envy?

Alas! I can still recall the delicious sensation of paddling across the smooth sea-sand, and of walking up the bed of a Highland burn. But "Oh! the change twixt' Now and Then," I sat calmly on a stone, dry-shod; as was best. Still, is it not a benign law of nature, that the things we are no longer able to do, we almost cease to wish to do? Perhaps even the last cessation of all things will come naturally at the end, as naturally as we turn round and go to sleep at night?

But it was not night yet. I am proud to think how high and steep was the cliff we re-ascended, all three of us, and from which we stood and looked at sky and sea. Such a sea and such a sky : amber clear, so that one could trace the whole line of coast—Mount's Bay, with St. Michael's Mount dotted in the midst of it, and even the Land's End, beyond which the sun, round and red, was just touching the top of the waves. We should have liked to watch him drop below them—that splendid sea-sunset of which one never tires, but we had some distance to walk, and we began to rejoice in the prospect of Mary Mundy's tea.

"I'll go on ahead and have the carriage ready," said the ever thoughtful Charles. "You can't miss your way, ladies. Just follow the hedges"—that tempting aerial promenade, to which we were now getting accustomed, becoming veritable Blondins in petticoats—"then cross the cornfield ; and take to the hedges again. You'll be at the farm-yard directly."

Not quite—for we lingered, tempted by the abundance of corn-flowers, of which we gathered, not handfuls but armfuls. When we reached it, what a picture of an English farm-yard it was ! With a regular old-fashioned English milk-maid—such as Izaak Walton would have loved to describe— sitting amidst her shining pails, her cows standing round her, meekly waiting their turn. Sleek, calm creatures they were, Juno-eyed and soft-skinned—of that peculiar shade of grey which I have seen only in Cornwall. And, being rather a connoisseur in cows, I have often amused myself to notice how the kine of each country have their own predominant colour, which seems to harmonise with its special landscape. The curious yellow tint of Highland cattle, the red, white, or brown of those of the midland counties, and the delicate grey of Cornish cows, alike suit the scene around them, and belong to it as completely as the dainty little Swiss herds do to their Alpine pastures, or the large, mild, cream-coloured oxen to the Campagna at Rome.

But we had to tear ourselves away from this Arcadia, for in the midst of the farm-yard appeared the carriage and Charles. So we jolted back— it seemed as if Cornish carriages and horses could go anywhere and over everything—to the Old Inn and Mary Mundy.

She *had* come home, and everything was right. As we soon found, everything and everybody was accustomed to be put to rights by Miss Mary Mundy.

She stood at the door to greet us—a bright, brown-faced little woman with the reddest of cheeks and the blackest of eyes ; I have no hesitation

A CRABBER'S HOLE, GERRAN'S BAY.

G

in painting her portrait here, as she is, so to speak, public property, known and respected far and wide.

"Delighted to see you, ladies; delighted to see any friends of the Professor's; and I hope you enjoyed the Cove, and that you're all hungry, and will find your tea to your liking. It's the best we can do; we're very homely folk here, but we try to make people comfortable," and so on and so on a, regular stream of chatty conversation, given in the strongest Cornish, with the kindliest of Cornish hearts, as she ushered us into a neat little parlour at the back of the inn.

There lay spread, not one of your dainty afternoon teas, with two or three wafery slices of bread and butter, but a regular substantial meal. Cheerful candles—of course in serpentine candlesticks—were already lit, and showed us the bright teapot full of that welcome drink to weary travellers, hot, strong and harmless; the gigantic home-baked loaf, which it seemed sacrilegious to have turned into toast; the rich, yellow butter—I am sure those lovely cows had something to do with it, and also with the cream, so thick that the spoon could almost have stood upright in it. Besides, there was a quantity of that delicious clotted cream, which here accompanies every meal and of which I had vainly tried to get the receipt, but was answered with polite scorn, "Oh, ma'am, it would be of no use to *you*: Cornish cream can only be made from Cornish cows!"

Whether this remarkable fact in natural history be true or not, let me record the perfection of Mary Mundy's cream, which, together with her jam and her marmalade, was a refection worthy of the gods.

She pressed us again and again to "have some more," and her charge for our magnificent meal was as small as her gratitude was great for the slight addition we made to it.

"No, I'll not say no, ma'am, it'll come in handy; us has got a young niece to bring up—my brother and me—please'm. Yes, I'm glad you came, and I hope you'll come again, please'm. And if you see the Professor, you'll tell him he's not forgotten, please'm.

This garniture of "please'm" at the end of every sentence reminded us of the Venetian "probbedirla," *per ubbedirla*, with which our gondolier Giovanna used to amuse us, often dragging it in in the oddest way. "Yes, the Signora will get a beautiful day, probbedirla," or "My wife has just lost her baby, probbedirla." Mary Mundy's "please'm" often came in with equal

G 2

incongruity, and her voluble tongue ran on nineteen to the dozen; but her talk was so shrewd and her looks so pleasant—once, no doubt, actually pretty, and still comely enough for a middle-aged woman—that we departed, fully agreeing with her admiring Professor that

> " The brightest thing on Cornish land
> Is the face of Miss Mary Mundy.

Recrossing Pradenack down in the dim light of a newly-risen moon, everything looked so solitary and ghostly that we started to see moving from behind a furz-bush, a mysterious figure, which crossed the road slowly, and stood waiting for us. Was it man or ghost, or—

Only a donkey! A ridiculous grey donkey. It might have been Tregeagle himself—Tregeagle, the grim mad-demon of Cornish tradition, once a dishonest steward, who sold his soul to the devil, and is doomed to keep on emptying Dozmare Pool, near St. Neots (the same mere wherein Excalibur was thrown), with a limpet-shell; and to spend his nights in other secluded places balancing interminable accounts, which are always just sixpence wrong.

Poor Tregeagle! I fear some of us, weak in arithmetic, had a secret sympathy for him! But we never met him—nor anything worse than that spectral donkey, looming large and placid against the level horizon.

Soon, " the stars came out by twos and threes,"—promising a fine night and finer morning, during which, while we were comfortably asleep, our good horse and man would be driving across this lonely region to Falmouth, in time to take the good people to church on Sunday morning.

" And we'll do it, too—don't you be anxious about us, ladies," insisted Charles. " I'll feed him well, and groom him well. I likes to take care of a good horse, and you'll see, he'll take no harm. I'll be back when you want me, at the week's end, or perhaps before then, with some party or other—we're always coming to the Lizard—and I'll just look in and see how you're getting on, and how you liked Kynance. But take care of the tide."

We thanked our kindly charioteer, bade him and his horse good-bye, wished him a pleasant journey through the moonlight, which was every minute growing more beautiful, then went indoors to supper—no! supper would have been an insult to Mary Mundy's tea—to bed.

DAY THE FOURTH

SUNDAY, September 4th—and we had started on September 1st; was it possible we had only been travelling four days?

It felt like fourteen at least. We had seen so much, taken in so many new interests—nay, made several new friends. Already we began to plan another meeting with John Curgenven, who we found was a relation of our landlady, or of our bright-faced serving maiden, Esther—I forget which. But everybody seemed connected with everybody at the Lizard, and everybody took a friendly interest in everybody. The arrival of new lodgers in the "genteel" parlour which we had not appreciated was important information, and we were glad to hear that Charles had started about four in the morning quite cheery.

And what a morning it was!—a typical Sabbath, a day of rest, a day to rejoice in. Strolling round the garden at eight o'clock, while the dew still lay thick on the grass, and glittered like diamonds on the autumnal spider-webs, even the flowers seemed to know it was Sunday, the mignonette bed to smell sweeter, the marigolds—yes! æsthetic fashion is right in its love for marigolds—burnt in a perfect blaze of golden colour and aromatic scent. The air was so mild that we could imagine summer was still with us: and the great wide circle of sea gleamed in the sunshine as if there never had been, never could be, such a thing as cloud or storm.

Having ascertained that there was no service nearer than Grade, some miles off, until the afternoon, we "went to church" on the cliffs, in Pistol Meadow, beside the green mounds where the two hundred drowned sailors sleep in peace.

And such a peaceful place! Absolutely solitary: not a living creature, not even a sheep came near me the whole morning:—and in the silence

STEAM SEINE BOATS GOING OUT.

I could hear almost every word said by my young folks, searching for sea-treasures among the rocks and little pools far below. Westwards towards Kynance, and eastwards towards Landewednack—the church we were to go to in the afternoon—the cliff path was smooth and green, the short grass full of those curious dainty flowers, some of which were new to our eager eyes. At other times the road was so precipitous that we did not wonder at those carefully white-washed stones every few yards, which are the sole guide to the coastguard men of dark nights. Even in daylight, if the wind were high, or the footing slippery with rain, the cliff-walk from the Lizard to Kynance would be no joke to uninitiated feet.

Now, all was so still that the wind never once fluttered the letter I was writing, and so warm that we were glad to escape the white glare of the wall of the Lizard Lights and sit in a cool hollow, watching sky and ocean, with now and then a sea-bird floating lazily between, a dark speck on the perpetual blue.

"If it will only keep like this all week!" And, as we sat, we planned out each day, so as to miss nothing, and lose nothing—either of time or strength: doing enough, but never too much—as is often the fatal mistake of tourists. And then, following the grand law of travelling, to have one's "meals reg'lar"—we went indoors and dined. Afterwards in honour of the day

> "that comes between
> The Saturday and Monday,"

we dressed ourselves in all our best—very humble best it was!—to join the good people going to church at Landewednack.

This, which in ancient Cornish means "the white-roofed church of St. Wednack"—hagiologists must decide who that individual was!—is the name of the parish to which the comparatively modern Lizard Town belongs. The church is in a very picturesque corner, close to the sea, though both it and the rectory are protected by a sudden dip in the ground, so that you see neither till you are close upon them. A fine Norman doorway, a curious hagioscope, and other points, interesting to archæologists—also the neatest and prettiest of churchyards—make note-worthy this, the most southerly church in England. A fine old building, not spoiled though "restored." The modern open pews, and a modern memorial pulpit of serpentine, jarred less than might have been expected with the carefully-preserved remains of the past.

In Landewednack church is said to have been preached the last sermon in Cornish. This was in 1678. Since, the ancient tongue has completely died out, and the people of King Arthur's country have become wholly English.

Still, they are not the English of the midland and northern districts, but of a very different type and race. I have heard it said that a sea-board population, accustomed to wrestle with the dangers of the coast, to move about from place to place, see foreign countries, and carry on its business in the deep waters, is always more capable, more intelligent, as a whole, than an inland people, whether agricultural or manufacturing. It may be so: but certainly the aborigines of Lizard Town, who could easily be distinguished from the visitors—of whom there was yet a tolerable sprinkling—made a very interesting congregation; orderly, respectable, reverent; simple in dress and manner, yet many of them, both the men and women, exceedingly picturesque. That is, the old men and the old women: the younger ones aped modern fashion even here, in this out-of-the-way corner, and consequently did not look half so well as their seniors.

I must name one more member of the congregation—a large black dog, who walked in and settled himself in the pew behind, where he behaved during half the service in an exemplary manner, worthy of the Highland shepherds' dogs, who always come to church with their masters, and conduct themselves with equal decorum.

There is always a certain pathos in going in to worship in a strange church, with a strange congregation, of whom you are as ignorant as they of you. In the intervals of kneeling with them as "miserable sinners," one finds oneself speculating upon them, their possible faults and virtues, joys and sorrows, hopes and fears, watching the unknown faces, and trying to read thereon the records of a common humanity. A silent homily, better perhaps than most sermons.

Not that there was aught to complain of in the sermon, and the singing was especially good. Many a London choir might have taken a lesson from this village church at the far end of Cornwall. When service was over, we lingered in the pretty and carefully tended churchyard, where the evening light fell softly upon many curious gravestones, of seafaring men, and a few of wrecked sailors—only a few, since it is but within a generation that bodies washed ashore from the deep were allowed to be buried in consecrated ground; most of them, like the two hundred in Pistol Meadow, being interred as near as convenient to where they were found, without any burial rites.   Still, in all the churchyards along this coast are graves with a story.   A little corner railed off has an old and sad one. There lie buried the victims of the plague, which in 1645 devastated the village.   No one since has ever ventured to disturb their resting-place.

Very green and peaceful the churchyard looked : the beautiful day was dying, beautiful to the last.   We stood and watched the congregation melt slowly away, disappearing down the lane, and then, attracted by the sound of music, we re-entered the church.   There we sat and listened for another half-hour to the practising of an anthem ready for the harvest festival, which had been announced for the following Tuesday ; exceedingly well done too, the rector's voice leading it all, with an energy and enthusiasm that at once accounted for the capital condition of the choir.

"If this weather will only last!" was our earnest sigh as we walked home ; and anxious not to lose a minute of it, we gave ourselves the briefest rest, and turned out again, I to watch the sunset from the cliffs, while the others descended once more to their beloved sea-pools.

"Such anemones, such sea-weed! and scrambling is so delicious! Besides, sunsets are all alike," added the youthful, practical, and slightly unpoetical mind.

No, they are not alike.   Every one has a mysterious charm of its own—just like that in every new human face.   I have seen hundreds of sunsets in my time, and those I shall see are narrowing down now, but I think to the end of my life I shall always feel a day incomplete of which I did not see the sunset.

This one was splendid.   The usual place where the sun dropped into the sea, just beyond the point of the Land's End, was all a golden mist.   I hastened west, climbing one intervening cliff after the other, anxious not to miss the clear sight of him as he set his glowing feet, or rather his great round disc, on the sea.   At last I found a "comfortable" stone, sheltered from the wind, which blew tolerably fresh, and utterly solitary (as I thought), the intense silence being such that one could almost hear the cropping of three placid sheep—evidently well accustomed to sunsets, and thinking them of little consequence.

There I sat until the last red spark had gone out, quenched in the Atlantic waters, and from behind the vanished sun sprung a gleam of absolutely green light, "like a firework out of a rocket," the young people

II

said; such as I had never seen before, though we saw it once afterwards. Nature's fireworks they were; and I could see even the two little black figures moving along the rocks below stand still to watch them. I watched too, with that sort of lonely delight—the one shadow upon it being that it is so lonely—with which all one's life one is accustomed to watch beautiful and vanishing things. Then seeing how fast the colours were fading and

HAULING IN THE BOATS—EVENING.

the sky darkening, I rose; but just took a step or two farther to look over the edge of my stone into the next dip of the cliff, and there I saw—

Actually, two human beings! Lovers, of course. Nothing else would have sat so long and so silently, for I had been within three yards of them all the time, and had never discovered them, nor they me. Poor young things! they did not discover me even yet. They sat, quite absorbed in one another, hand in hand, looking quietly seaward, their faces bathed in the rosy sunset—which to them was a sunrise, the sort of sun which never rises twice in a life-time.

I left them to it. Evidently they did not see me, in fact I just peered over the rock's edge and drew back again ; any slight sound they probably attributed to the harmless sheep. Well, it was but an equally harmless old woman, who did not laugh at them, as some might have done, but smiled and wished them well, as she left them to their sunset, and turned to face the darkening east, where the sun would rise to-morrow.

The moon was rising there now, and it was a picture to behold. Indeed, all these Cornish days seemed so full of moonrises and sunsets—and sun-rises too—that it was really inconvenient. Going to bed seemed almost a sin—as on this night, when, opening our parlour door, which looked right on to the garden, we saw the whole world lying in a flood of moonlight peace, the marigolds and carnations leaning cheek to cheek, as motionless as the two young lovers on the cliff. Who, alas! must long ago have had their dream broken, for five minutes afterwards I had met a most respectable fat couple from Lizard Town taking their Sunday evening stroll, in all their Sunday best, along those very cliffs. Most painful interruption! But perhaps, the good folks had once been lovers too.

What a night it was! fit night to such a perfect day. How the stars shone, without a mist or a cloud ; how the Lizard Lights gleamed, even in spite of the moonlight, and how clear showed the black outline of Kynance Cove, from which came through the silence a dull murmur of waves! It was, as we declared, a sin and a shame to go to bed at all though we had been out the whole day, and hoped to be out the whole of to-morrow. Still, human nature could not keep awake for ever. We passed from the poetical to the practical, and decided to lay us down and sleep.

But, in the middle of the night I woke, rose, and looked out of the window.

What a change! Sea and sky were one blackness, literally as " black as ink," and melting into one another so that both were undistinguishable. As for the moon and stars—heaven knows where they had gone to, for they seemed utterly blotted out. The only light visible was the ghostly gleam of those two great eyes, the Lizard Lights, stretching far out into

H 2

the intense darkness. I never saw such darkness—unbroken even by the white crest of a wave. And the stillness was like the stillness of death, with a heavy weight in the air which made me involuntarily go to sleep again, though with an awed impression of "something going to happen."

And sure enough in another hour something did happen. I started awake, feeling as if a volley of artillery had been poured in at my window. It was the wildest deluge of rain, beating against the panes, and with it came a wind that howled and shrieked round the house as if all the demons in Cornwall, Tregeagle himself included, were let loose at once.

Now we understood what a Lizard storm could be. I have seen Mediterranean storms, sweeping across the Campagna like armed battalions of avenging angels, pouring out their vials of wrath—rain, hail, thunder, and lightning—unceasingly for two whole days. I have been in Highland storms, so furious that one had to sit down in the middle of the road with one's plaid over one's head, till the worst of their rage was spent. But I never saw or heard anything more awful than this Lizard storm, to which I lay and listened till the day began to dawn.

Then the wind lulled a little, but the rain still fell in torrents, and the sky and sea were as black as ever. The weather had evidently broken for good—that is, for evil. Alas! the harvest, and the harvest festival! And alas—of minor importance, but still some, to us at least— alas for our holiday in Cornwall! Only four days, and—this!

It was with a heavy heart that, feeling there was not the slightest use in getting up, I turned round and took another sleep.

DAY THE FIFTH

"HOPE for the best, and be prepared for the worst," had been the motto of our journey. So when we rose to one of the wettest mornings that ever came out of the sky, there was a certain satisfaction in being prepared for it.

"We must have a fire, that is certain," was our first decision. This entailed the abolition of our beautiful decorations—our sea-holly and ferns; also some anxious looks from our handmaiden. Apparently no fire had been lit in this rather despised room for many months—years perhaps—and the chimney rather resented being used. A few agonised down-puffs greatly interfered with the comfort of the breakfast table, and an insane attempt to open the windows made matters worse.

Which was most preferable—to be stifled or deluged? We were just considering the question, when the chimney took a new and kinder thought, or the wind took a turn—it seemed to blow alternately from every quarter, and then from all quarters at once—the smoke went up straight, the room grew warm and bright, with the cosy peace of the first fire of the season. Existence became once more endurable, nay, pleasant.

"We shall survive, spite of the rain!" And we began to laugh over our lost day which we had meant to begin by bathing in Housel Cove; truly, just to stand outside the door would give an admirable douche bath in three minutes. "But how nice it is to be inside, with a roof over our heads, and no necessity for travelling. Fancy the unfortunate tourists who have fixed on to-day for visiting the Lizard!" (Charles had told us that Monday was a favourite day for excursions.) "Fancy anybody being obliged to go out such weather as this!"

And in our deep pity for our fellow-creatures we forgot to pity ourselves.

Nor was there much pity needed ; we had provided against emergencies, with a good store of needlework and knitting, anything that would pack in small compass, also a stock of unquestionably "light" literature—paper-covered, double-columned, sixpenny volumes, inclosing an amount of enjoyment which those only can understand who are true lovers of Walter Scott. We had enough of him to last for a week of wet days. And we had a one-volume Tennyson, all complete, and a " Morte d'Arthur "—Sir Thomas Malory's. On this literary provender we felt that as yet we should not starve.

Also, some little fingers having a trifling turn for art, brought out triumphantly a colour-box, pencils, and pictures. And the wall-paper being one of the very ugliest that ever eye beheld, we sought and obtained permission to adorn it with these, our *chefs-d'œuvre*, pasted at regular intervals. Where we hope they still remain, for the edification of succeeding lodgers.

We read the " Idylls of the King " all through, finishing with " The Passing of Arthur," where the " bold Sir Bedivere " threw Excalibur into the mere—which is supposed to be Dozmare Pool. Here King Arthur's faithful lover was so melted—for the hundredth time—by the pathos of the story, and by many old associations, that the younger and more practical minds grew scornful, and declared that probably King Arthur had never existed at all—or if he had, was nothing but a rough barbarian, unlike even the hero of Sir Thomas Malory, and far more unlike the noble modern gentleman of Tennyson's verse. Maybe : and yet, seeing that

> "'Tis better to have loved and lost
> Than never to have loved at all,"

may it not be better to have believed in an impossible ideal man, than to accept contentedly a low ideal, and worship blindly the worldly, the mean, or the base ?

This topic furnished matter for so much hot argument, that, besides doing a quantity of needlework, we succeeded in making our one wet day by no means the least amusing of our seventeen days in Cornwall.

HAULING IN THE LINES.

Hour after hour we watched the rain—an even down-pour. In the midst of it we heard a rumour that Charles had been seen about the town, and soon after he appeared at the door, hat in hand, soaked but smiling, to inquire for and sympathise with his ladies. Yes, he *had* brought a party to the Lizard that day!—unfortunate souls (or bodies), for there could not have been a dry thread left on them! We gathered closer round our cosy fire; ate our simple dinner with keen enjoyment, and agreed that after all we had much to be thankful for.

In the afternoon the storm abated a little, and we thought we would seize the chance of doing some shopping, if there was a shop in Lizard Town. So we walked—I ought rather to say waded, for the road was literally swimming—meeting not one living creature, except a family of young ducks, who, I need scarcely say, were enjoying supreme felicity.

"Yes, ladies, this is the sort of weather we have pretty well all winter. Very little frost or snow, but rain and storm, and plenty of it. Also fogs; I've heard there's nothing anywhere like the fogs at the Lizard."

So said the woman at the post-office, which, except the serpentine shops, seemed to be the one emporium of commerce in the place. There we could get all we wanted, and a good deal that we were very thankful we did not want, of eatables, drinkables, and wearables. Also ornaments, china vases, &c., of a kind that would have driven frantic any person of æsthetic tastes. Among them an active young Cornishman of about a year old was meandering aimlessly, or with aims equally destructive to himself and the community. He all but succeeded in bringing down a row of plates upon his devoted head, and then tied himself up, one fat finger after another, in a ball of twine, upon which he began to howl violently.

"He's a regular little trial," said the young mother proudly. "He's only sixteen months old, and yet he's up to all sorts of mischief. I don't know what in the world I shall do with he, presently. Naughty boy!" with a delighted scowl.

"Not naughty, only active," suggested another maternal spirit, and pleaded that the young jackanapes should be found something to do that was not mischief, but yet would occupy his energies, and fill his mind. At which, the bright bold face looked up as if he had understood it all—an absolutely fearless face, brimming with fun, and shrewdness too. Who knows? The "regular little trial" may grow into a valuable member of society—fisherman, sailor, coastguardman—daring and doing heroic deeds;

I

perhaps saving many a life on nights such as last night, which had taught us what Cornish coast-life was all winter through.

The storm was now gradually abating; the wind had lulled entirely, the rain had ceased, and by sunset a broad yellow streak all along the west implied that it might possibly be a fine day to-morrow.

But the lane was almost a river still, and the slippery altitudes of the "hedges" were anything but desirable. As the only possible place for a walk I ventured into a field where two or three cows cropped their supper of damp grass round one of those green hillocks seen in every Cornish pasture field—a manure heap planted with cabbages, which grow there with a luxuriance that turns ugliness into positive beauty. Very dreary everything was—the soaking grass, the leaden sky, the angry-looking sea, over which a rainy moon was just beginning to throw a faint glimmer; while shorewards one could just trace the outline of Lizard Point and the wheat-field behind it. Yesterday those fields had looked so sunshiny and fair, but to-night they were all dull and grey, with rows of black dots indicating the soppy, sodden harvest sheaves.

Which reminded me that to-morrow was the harvest festival at Landewednack, when all the world and his wife was invited by shilling tickets to have tea in the rectory garden, and afterwards to assist at the evening thanksgiving service in the church.

"Thanksgiving! What for?" some poor farmer might well exclaim, especially on such a day as this. Some harvest festivals must occasionally seem a bitter mockery. Indeed, I doubt if the next generation will not be wise in taking our "Prayers for Rain," "Prayers for Fair Weather," clean out of the liturgy. Such conceited intermeddling with the government of the world sounds to some ridiculous, to others actually profane. "Snow and hail, mists and vapours, wind and storm, fulfilling His Word." And it must be fulfilled, no matter at what cost to individuals or to nations. The laws of the universe must be carried out, even though the mystery of sorrow, like the still greater mystery of evil, remains for ever unexplained. "Shall not the Judge of all the earth do right?"

And how right is His right! How marvellously beautiful He can make this world! until we can hardly imagine anything more beautiful in the world everlasting. Ay, even after such a day as to-day, when the world seems hardly worth living in, yet we live on, live to wake up unto such a to-morrow—

But I must wait to speak of it in another page.

DAY THE SIXTH

ND a day absolutely divine! Not a cloud upon the sky, not a ripple upon the water, or it appeared so in the distance. Nearer, no doubt, there would have been that heavy ground-swell which is so long in subsiding, in fact is scarcely ever absent on this coast. The land, like the sea, was all one smile; the pasture fields shone in brilliant green, the cornfields gleaming yellow—at once a beauty and a thanksgiving.

It was the very perfection of an autumn morning. We would not lose an hour of it, but directly after breakfast started leisurely to find Housel Cove and try our first experiment of bathing in the wide Atlantic.

The Atlantic it certainly was. Not a rood of land lay between us and America. Yet the illimitable ocean "where the great ships go down," rolled in to our feet in baby ripples, disporting itself harmlessly, and tempting my two little mermaids to swim out to the utmost limit that prudence allowed. And how delightful it was to run back barefoot across the soft sand to the beautiful dressing-room of serpentine rock, where one could sit and watch the glittering sea, untroubled by any company save the gulls and cormorants. What a contrast to other bathing places—genteel Eastbourne and Brighton, or vulgar Margate and Ramsgate, where, nevertheless, the good folks look equally happy. But our happiness! No words could describe it. Shall we stamp ourselves as persons of little mind, easily satisfied, if I confess that we spent the whole morning in Housel Cove without band or promenade, without even a Christy Minstrel or a Punch and Judy, our sole amusement being the vain attempt to catch a tiny fish, the Robinson Crusoe of a small pool in the rock above high-water mark, where

I 2

by some ill chance he found himself.   But he looked extremely contented
with his sea hermitage, and evaded so cleverly all our efforts to get hold of
him, that after a while we left him to his solitude—where possibly
he resides still.

    How delicious it is for hard-worked people to do nothing, absolutely
nothing! Of course only for a little while—a few days, a few hours.   The
love of work and the necessity for it soon revive.   But just for those few

THE LIZARD LIGHTS BY DAY.

harmless hours to let the world and its duties and cares alike slip by, to be
absolutely idle, to fold one's hands and look at the sea and the sky, thinking
of nothing at all, except perhaps to count and watch for every ninth wave—
said to be the biggest always—and wonder how big it will be, and whether
it will reach that stone with the little colony of limpets and two red anemones
beside them, or stop short at the rock where we sit placidly dangling our
feet, waiting, Canute-like, for the supreme moment when the will of humanity

sinks conquered by the immutable powers of nature. Then, greatest crisis of all, the sea will attack that magnificent castle and moat, which we grown-up babies have constructed with such pride. Well, have we not all built our sand-castles and seen them swept away? happy if by no unkinder force than the remorseless wave of Time, which will soon flow over us all.

But how foolish is moralising—making my narrative halt like that horse whom we amused ourselves with half the afternoon. He was tied by the leg, poor beast, the fore leg fastened to the hind one, as seemed to be the ordinary Cornish fashion with all animals—horses, cows, and sheep. It certainly saves a deal of trouble, preventing them from climbing the "hedges" which form the sole boundary of property, but it makes the creatures go limping about in rather a melancholy fashion. However, as it is their normal condition, probably they communicate it to one another, and each generation accepts its lot.

This horse did. He was a handsome animal, who came and peered at the sketch which one of us was doing, after the solemn fashion of quadrupedal connoisseurship, and kept us company all the afternoon. We sat in a row on the top of the "hedge," enjoying the golden afternoon, and scarcely believing it possible that yesterday had been yesterday. Of the wild storm and deluge of rain there was not a single trace; everything looked as lovely as if it had been, and was going to be, summer all the year.

We were so contented, and were making such progress in our sketch and distant view of Kynance over the now dry and smiling cornfield, that we had nigh forgotten the duties of civilisation, until some one brought the news that all the household was apparently dressing itself in its very best, to attend the rectory tea. We determined to do the same, though small were our possibilities of toilette.

"But what does it matter?" argued we. "Nobody knows us, and we know nobody."

A position rather rare to those who "dwell among their own people," who take a kindly interest in everybody, and believe with a pardonable credulity that everybody takes a kindly interest in them.

But human nature is the same all the world over. And here we saw it in its pleasantest phase; rich and poor meeting together, not for charity, but courtesy—a courtesy that was given with a kindliness and accepted with a quiet independence which seemed characteristic of these Cornish folk.

Among the little crowd, gentle and simple, we, of course, did not know a single soul. Nevertheless, delivering up our tickets to the gardener at the gate, we entered, and wandered at ease through the pretty garden, gorgeous with asters, marigolds, carnations, and all sorts of rich-coloured and rich-scented autumn flowers; where the hydrangeas grew in enormous bushes, and the fuchsias had stems as thick and solid as trees.

In front of the open hall door was a gravel sweep where were ranged two long tea-tables filled with the humbler but respectable class of parishioners, chiefly elderly people, and some very old. The Lizard is a place noted for longevity, as is proved by the register books, where several deaths at over a hundred may be found recorded, and one—he was the rector of Landewednack in 1683—is said to have died at the age of 120 years.

The present rector is no such Methuselah. He moved actively to and fro among his people, and so did his wife, whom we should have recognised by her omnipresent kindliness, even if she had not come and welcomed us strangers—easily singled out as strangers, where all the rest were friends.

Besides the poor and the aged, there was a goodly number of guests who were neither the one nor the other, playing energetically at lawn-tennis behind the house, on a "lawn" composed of sea-sand. All seemed determined to amuse themselves and everybody else, and all did their very best—including the band.

Alas, that band! I would fain pass it over in silence (would it had returned the compliment!); but truth is truth, and may benefit rather than harm. The calm composure with which those half-dozen wind-instruments sat in a row, playing determinedly flat, bass coming in with a tremendous boom here and there, entirely at his own volition, without regard to time or tune, was the most awful thing I ever heard in music! Agony, pure and simple, was the only sensation it produced. When they struck up, we just ran away till the tune was ended—what tune, familiar or unfamiliar, it was impossible to say. Between us three, all blessed, or cursed, with musical ears, there existed such difference of opinion on this head, that decision became vain. And when at last, as the hour of service approached, little groups began strolling towards the church, the musicians began a final "God save the Queen," barely recognisable, a feeling of thankfulness was the only sensation left.

Now, let me not be hard upon these village Orpheuses. They did

THE FISHERMAN'S DAUGHTER—A CORNISH STUDY.

their best, and for a working man to study music in any form is a good and desirable thing. But whatever is worth doing at all is worth doing well. The great bane of provincial life is that people have so few opportunities of finding out when they do *not* do things well, and so little ambition to learn to do them better. If these few severe remarks should spur on that anonymous band to try and emulate the Philharmonic or the Crystal Palace orchestra, it will be all the better for the little community at the Lizard.

The music in the church was beautiful. A crowded congregation—not a seat vacant—listened to the excellent chanting, hymns, and a harvest anthem, most accurately and correctly sung. The organist too—it was a pleasure to watch that young man's face and see with what interest and enthusiasm he entered into it all. Besides the rector, there were several other clergymen, one of whom, an old man, read the prayers with an intonation and expression which I have rarely heard equalled, and another preached what would have been called anywhere a thoroughly good sermon. All the statelier guests at the Rectory tea—probably county families (one stout lady had the dignity of a duchess at least)—"assisted" at this evening service, and behind them was a throng of humbler folk, among whom we recognised our sole friend here, John Curgenven. We had passed him at the church door, and he had lifted his hat with the air of a *preux chevalier* of the olden time; "more like King Arthur than ever"—we observed to one another.

He, and we, and the aristocratic groups, with a few more of the congregation, lingered for several minutes after service was over, admiring the beautiful flowers and fruit. I think I never saw any decorations so rich or so tasteful. And then, as the organ played us out with an exceedingly brilliant voluntary, the vision of light and colour melted away, and we came out upon the quiet churchyard, lying in the cold, still moonlight.

But what a moonlight! Clear as day, the round silver orb sailing through a cloudless sky of that deep dark which we know is blue, only moonlight shows no colours. Oh, Lady Moon, Lady Moon, what a dangerous night for some of those groups to go walking home in! We saw them in twos and threes, various young people whom we had got to know by sight, and criticise, and take an interest in, wandering slowly on through Lizard Town, and then diverging into quieter paths.

As we gladly did too. For there, in an open space near the two hotels

K

which co-exist close together—I hope amicably, and divide the tourist custom
of the place—in front of a row of open windows which showed the remains
of a *table d'hôte*, and playing lively tunes to a group of delighted listeners,
including some children, who had struck up a merry dance—stood that
terrible wind band!

It was too much! All our sympathy with our fellow-creatures, our
pleasure in watching them enjoy themselves, our interest in studying human
nature in the abstract, nay, even the picturesqueness of the charming
moonlight scene, could not tempt us to stay. We paused a minute, then
put our fingers in our ears and fled. Gradually those fearful sounds melted
away into distance, and left us to the silence of moonshine, and the
sight, now grown familiar, but never less beautiful, of the far-gleaming
Lizard Lights.

DAY THE SEVENTH

JOHN CURGENVEN had said last night, with his air of tender patronising, half regal, half paternal, which we declared always reminded us of King Arthur — "Ladies, whenever you settle to go to Kynance, I'll take you."

And sure enough there he stood, at eight in the morning, quite a picture, his cap in one hand, a couple of fishes dangling from the other—he had brought them as a present, and absolutely refused to be paid—smiling upon us at our breakfast, as benignly as did the sun. He came to say that he was at our service till 10 A.M.; when he had an engagement.

Our countenances fell. We did not like venturing in strange and dangerous ground, or rather sea, without our protector. But this was our last chance, and such a lovely day.

"You won't come to any harm, ladies," said the consoling John. "I'll take you by a·short cut across the down, much better than the cliff. You can't possibly miss your way: it'll lead you straight to Kynance, and then you go down a steep path to the Cove. You'll have plenty of time before the tide comes in to see everything."

"And to bathe?"

"Oh yes, miss, there's the Drawing-room, the Dining-room, and the Kitchen—all capital caves close together; I wouldn't advise you to swim out far, though. And keep a sharp look out for the tide—it runs in pretty fast."

"And the scrambling?"

"Oh, you can easy get on Asparagus Island, miss; it's quite safe. Only don't try the Devil's Throat—or Hell's Mouth, as some folk call it."

K 2

Neither name was inviting; but studying our guide-books, we thought we could manage even without our friend. So, long ere the dew was dried on the sunshiny down, we all started off together, Curgenven slackening his quick active steps—very light and most enviably active for a man of his years—to accommodate us, and conversing courteously with us all the way.

"Ower the muir amang the heather" have I tramped many a mile in bonnie Scotland, but this Cornish moor and Cornish heather were quite

KYNANCE COVE, CORNWALL.

different. As different as the Cornishman with his bright, frank face, and his mixture of British honesty and Gallic courtesy, from the Scotch peasant —equally worthy, but sometimes just a trifle "dour."

John had plenty to say for himself, and said it well, with a quiet independence that there was no mistaking; never forgetting meanwhile to stop and offer a helping hand over every bit of rough road, puddle, or bog. He gave us a vivid picture of winter life at the Lizard: when the little community has to hybernate, like the squirrels and field-mice, upon its summer savings.

"Sometimes we don't earn a halfpenny for weeks and months, and then if we've got nothing to fall back upon it's a bad job, you see, ma'am."

I asked him if much money went for drink; they seemed to me a remarkably sober set at the Lizard.

"Yes, I think we are; we're obliged to be; we can't spend money at the public-house, for we've got none to spend. I'm no teetotaller myself," added John boldly. "I don't dislike a glass of beer now and then, if I can afford it, and when I can't afford it I can do without it, and if I do take it I always know when to stop."

Ay, that is the crucial test—the knowing when to stop. It is this which makes all the difference between a good man and a villain, a wise man and a fool. Self-control—a quality which, guided by conscience and common sense, is the best possession of any human being. And looking at the honest fisherman, one felt pretty sure he had his share of it.

"Now I must leave you, ladies," said he, a great deal sooner than we wished, for we much liked talking to him. "My time's nearly up, and I mustn't keep my gentleman waiting; he goes out in my boat every day, and has been a good friend to me. The road's straight before you, ladies; and there's another party just ahead of you. Follow the track, and you'll soon be at Kynance. It's a lovely day for the Cove, and I hope you'll enjoy yourselves."

John bared his grey head, with a salutation worthy of some old knight of the Round Table, and then strode back, in double-quick time, as active and upright as any young fellow of twenty-five, across the level down.

Beautiful Kynance! When, afterwards, I stood one dull winter day in a London Art Gallery, opposite the *Cornish Lions*, how well I recalled this day! How truly Brett's picture gives the long roll of the wave upon the silver sands, the richly-tinted rocks and caves, the brightness and freshness of everything. And those merry girls beside me, who had the faculty of enjoying all they had, and all they did, without regretting what they had not or what they might not do—with heroic resignation they promised not to attempt to swim in the tempting smooth water beyond the long rollers. Though knocked down again and again, they always emerged from the waves with shouts of laughter. Mere dots they looked to my anxious eyes

—a couple of corks tossed hither and thither on the foaming billows—and very thankful I was to get them safe back into the "drawing-room," the loveliest of lovely caves.

There was no time to lose; by noon our parlour floor—what a fairy floor it was! of the softest, most delicious sand—would be all covered with waves. And before then there was a deal to be seen and done, the Bellows, the Gull Rock, Asparagus Island—even if we left out the dangerous points with the ugly names that Curgenven had warned us against.

What is there in humanity, certainly in youthful humanity, that if it can attain its end in two ways, one quiet and decorous, the other difficult and dangerous, is certain to choose the latter?

"We must manage to get you to the Bellows, it is such a curious sight," said my girls as they returned from it. "Don't be frightened—come along!"

By dint of pulling, pushing, and the help of stick and arm, I came: stood watching the spout of water which, in certain conditions of the tide, forces itself through a tiny fissure in the rock with a great roar, and joined in the childish delight of waiting, minute by minute, for the biggest spout, the loudest roar.

But Asparagus Island (where was no asparagus at all) I totally declined. Not being a goat or a chamois, I contented myself with sitting where I could gain the best view of the almost invisible path by which my adventurous young "kids" disappeared. Happily they had both steady heads and cool nerves; they were neither rash nor unconscientious. I knew they would come back as soon as they could. So I waited patiently, contemplating a fellow-victim who seemed worse off than myself; a benign-looking clergyman, who kept walking up and down the soppy sands, and shouting at intervals to two young people, a man and a woman, who appeared to be crawling like flies along the face of the rock towards another rock, with a yawning cave and a wide fissure between.

"Don't attempt it!" the clergyman cried at the top of his voice. "That's the Devil's Throat. She'll never manage it. Come down. Do make her come down."

"Your young people seem rather venturesome," said I sympathetically.

"Not *my* young people," was the dignified answer. "My girls are up there, on Asparagus Rock, which is easy enough climbing. They promised not to go farther, and they never disobey their mother and me. But those two! I declare he is taking her to the most dangerous part, that rock

THE STEEPLE ROCK, KYNANCE COVE.

where you have to jump—a good jump it is, and if you miss your footing you are done for, you go right into the boiling waves below.

Well, it's no business of mine; she is his own property; he is engaged to her, but "—

I fear I made some very severe remarks on the folly of a young man who could thus risk life and limbs—not only his own, but those of his wife to be; and on the weakness of a girl who could allow herself to be tempted, even by a lover, into such selfish foolhardiness.

"They must manage their own affairs," said the old gentleman sententiously, perhaps not being so much given to preaching (out of the pulpit) as I was. "My daughters are wiser. Here come two of them."

And very sensible girls they looked, clad in a practical, convenient fashion, just fitted for scrambling. By them I sent a message to my own girls, explaining the best descent from Asparagus Island, and repeating the warning against attempting Hell's Mouth.

"Yes, you are quite right," said my elderly friend, as we sat down together on the least uncomfortable stone we could find, and watched the juniors disappear over the rocks. "I like to see girls active and brave; I never hinder them in any reasonable enjoyment, even though there may be risk in it—one must run some risk—and a woman may have to save life as well as a man. But foolhardy bravado I not only dislike—I *despise* it."

In which sentiments I so entirely agreed that we fraternised there and then; began talking on all sorts of subjects—some of them the very serious and earnest subjects that one occasionally drops into by mere chance, with mere strangers. I recall that half hour on Kynance Sands as one of the pleasant memories of our tour, though to this day I have not the remotest idea who my companion was. Except that as soon as he spoke I recognised the reader whose voice had so struck me in last night's thanksgiving service; reminding me of Frederick Denison Maurice, whom this generation is almost beginning to forget, but whom we elders never can forget.

The tide was creeping on now—nay, striding, wave after wave, through "parlour" and "drawing-room," making ingress and egress alike impossible. In fact, a newly arrived party of tourists, who had stood unwisely long contemplating the Bellows, were seen to gaze in despair from their rock which had suddenly become an island. No chance for them except to wade—and in a few minutes more they would probably have to swim ashore. What became of them we did not stay to see, for an anxious, prudent little voice, always thoughtful for "mother," insisted on our precipitate flight before the advancing tide. Kynance, lovely as it is, has its inconveniences.

Departing, we met a whole string of tourist-looking people, whom we benevolently warned that they were too late, at which they did not seem in the least disappointed. Probably they were one of the numerous pic-nic parties who come here from Falmouth or Helstone, to spend a jovial day of eating and drinking, and enjoy the delights of the flesh rather than the spirit.

At any rate the romance and solitude of the place were gone. The quaint old woman at the serpentine shop—a mild little wooden erection under the cliff—was being chaffed and bargained with by three youths with cigars, which defiled the whole air around, and made us take refuge up the hill. But even there a white umbrella had sprung up like a gigantic mushroom, and under it sat an energetic lady artist, who, entering at once into conversation, with a cheerful avidity that implied her not having talked for a week, informed us of all she was painting, and all she had meant to paint, where she lodged, and how much she paid for her lodging—evidently expecting the same confidences from us in return.

But we were getting hungry, and between us and dinner was a long two-miles walk over the steep downs, that were glowing, nay, burning, under the September sun. So we turned homeward, glad of more than one rest by the way, and a long pause beside a pretty little stream ; where we were able to offer the immemorial cup of cold water to several thirsty souls besides ourselves. Some of us by this time were getting to feel not so young as we had fancied ourselves in the early morning, and to wish regretfully for Charles and his carriage.

However, we got home at last—to find that sad accompaniment of many a holiday—tidings of sickness and death. Nothing very near us— nothing that need hurry us home—but enough to sadden us, and make our evening walk, which we bravely carried out, a far less bright one than that of the forenoon.

The girls had found a way, chiefly on the tops of "hedges," to the grand rock called Lizard Point. Thither we went, and watched the sunset —a very fine one ; then came back through the village, and made various purchases of serpentine from John Curgenven's wife, who was a great deal younger than himself, but not near so handsome or so original.

But a cloud had come over us; it did not, and must not stay—still, there it was for the time. When the last thing at night I went out into the glorious moonlight—bright as day—and thought of the soul who had just passed out of a long and troubled life into the clearness of life eternal, it seemed as if all was right still. Small cares and worries dwindled down or melted away—as the petty uglinesses around melted in the radiance of this glorious harvest moon, which seemed to wrap one round in a silent peace, like the " garment of praise," which David speaks about—in exchange for " the spirit of heaviness."

DAY THE EIGHTH

AND seven days were all we could allow ourselves at the Lizard, if we meant to see the rest of Cornwall. We began to reckon with sore hearts that five days were already gone, and it seemed as if we had not seen half we ought to see, even of our near surroundings.

"We will take no excursion to-day. We will just have our bath at Housel Cove and then we will wander about the shore, and examine the Lizard Lights. Only fancy, our going away to-morrow without having seen the inside of the Lizard Lights! Oh, I wish we were not leaving so soon. We shall never like any place as we like the Lizard."

It was indeed very delightful. Directly after breakfast—and we are people who never vary from our eight o'clock breakfast, so that we always see the world in its early morning brightness and freshness—we went

"Brushing with hasty steps the dew away,"

along the fields, which led down to Housel or Househole Cove. Before us, clear in the sunshine, rose the fine headland of Penolver, and the green slopes of the amphitheatre of Belidden, supposed to be the remains of a Druidical temple. That, and the chair of Belidden, a recess in the rock, whence there is a splendid view, with various archæological curiosities, true or traditionary, we ought to have examined, I know. But—we didn t do it. Some of us were content to rejoice in the general atmosphere of beauty and peace without minute investigation, and some of us were so eminently practical that "a good bathe" appeared more important than all the poetry and archæology in the world.

So we wandered slowly on, rejoicing at having the place all to ourselves, when we came suddenly upon a tall black figure intently watching three other black figures, or rather dots, which were climbing slowly over Penolver.

It was our clerical friend of Kynance; with whom, in the natural and right civility of holiday-makers, we exchanged a courteous good morning.

THE LION ROCKS—A SEA IN WHICH NOTHING CAN LIVE.

"Yes, those are my girls up on the cliff there. They have been bathing, and are now going to walk to Cadgwith."

"Then nobody fell into the Devil's Throat at Kynance? They all came back to you with whole limbs?"

"Yes," said he smiling, "and they went again for another long walk in the afternoon. At night, when it turned out to be such splendid moonlight, they actually insisted on going launce-fishing. Of course you know about launce-fishing?"

I pleaded my utter ignorance of that noble sport.

"Oh, it is *the* thing at the Lizard. My boys—and girls too—consider it the best fun going. The launce is a sort of sand-eel peculiar to these coasts. It swims about all day, and at night burrows in the sand just above the waterline, where, when the moon shines on it, you can trace the silvery gleam of the creature. So you stand up to your ankles on wet sand, with a crooked iron spear which you dart in and hook him up, keeping your left hand free to seize him with."

"Easy fishing," said I, with a certain pity for the sand-eel.

"Not so easy as appears. You are apt either to chop him right in two, or miss him altogether, when off he wriggles in the sand and disappears. My young people say it requires a practised hand and a peculiar twist of the wrist, to have any success at all in launce fishing. It can only be done on moonlight nights—the full moon and a day or two after—and they are out half the night. They go about barefoot, which is much safer than soaked shoes and stockings. About midnight they light a fire on the sand, cook all the fish they have caught, and have a grand supper, as they had last night. They came home as merry as crickets about two o'clock this morning. Perhaps you might not have noticed what a wonderful moonlight night it was?"

I had; but it would not have occurred to me to spend it in standing for hours up to the knees in salt water, catching unfortunate fish.

However, tastes differ, and launce-fishing may be a prime delight to some people; so I faithfully chronicle it, and the proper mode of pursuing it, as one of the attractions at the Lizard. I am not aware that it is practised at any other part of the Cornish coast, nor can I say whether or not it was a pastime of King Arthur and his Knights. One cannot imagine Sir Tristram or Sir Launcelot occupied in spearing a small sand-eel.

The bathing at Housel Cove was delightful as ever. And afterwards we saw that very rare and beautiful sight, a perfect solar rainbow. Not the familiar bow of Noah, but a great luminous circle round the sun, like the halo often seen round the moon, extending over half the sky; yellow at first, then gradually assuming faint prismatic tints. This colouring, though never so bright as the ordinary arched rainbow, was wonderfully tender and delicate. We stood a long time watching it, till at last it melted slowly out of the sky, leaving behind a sense of mystery, as of something we had never seen before and might never see again in all our lives.

It was a lovely day, bright and warm as midsummer, tempting us to some distant excursion; but we had decided to investigate the Lizard Lights. We should have been content to take them for granted, in their purely poetical phase, as we had watched them night after night. But some of us were blessed with scientific relatives, who would have despised us utterly if we had spent a whole week at the Lizard and never gone to see the Lizard Lights. So we felt bound to do our duty, and admire, if we could not understand.

Which we certainly did not. I chronicle with shame that the careful and courteous explanations of that most intelligent young man, who met us at the door of the huge white building, apparently quite glad to have an opportunity of conducting us through it, were entirely thrown away. We mounted ladders, we looked at Brobdingnagian lamps, we poked into mysterious machinery for lighting them and for sounding the fog-horn, we listened to all that was told us, and tried to look as if we took it in. Very much interested we could not but be at such wonderful results of man's invention, but as for comprehending! we came away with our minds as dark as when we went in.

I have always found through life that, next to being clever, the safest thing is to know one's own ignorance and acknowledge it. Therefore let me leave all description of the astonishing mechanism of the Lizard Lights —I believe the first experiment of their kind, and not very long established —to abler pens and more intelligent brains. To see that young man, scarcely above the grade of a working man, handling his instruments and explaining them and their uses, seeming to take for granted that we could understand—which alas! we didn't, not an atom!—inspired me with a sense of humiliation and awe. Also of pride at the wonders this generation has accomplished, and is still accomplishing; employing the gradually comprehended forces of Nature against herself, as it were, and dominating her evil by ever-new discoveries and applications of the recondite powers of good.

The enormous body of light produced nightly—equal, I think he said, to 30,000 candles—and the complicated machinery for keeping the fog-horn continually at work, when even that gigantic blaze became invisible—all

HAULING IN THE BOATS.

this amount of skill, science, labour, and money, freely expended for the saving of life, gave one a strong impression of not only British power but British beneficence. Could King Arthur have come back again from his sea-engulfed Land of Lyonesse, and stood where we stood, beside the Lizard Lights, what would he have said to it all ?

Even though we did not understand, we were keenly interested in all we saw, and still more so in the stories of wrecks which this young man had witnessed even during the few years, or months—I forget which—of his stay at the Lizard. He, too, agreed, that the rocks there, called by the generic name of the Stags, were the most fatal of all on our coasts to ships outward and homeward bound. Probably because in the latter case, captain and crews get a trifle careless; and in the former—as I have heard in sad explanation of many emigrant ships being lost almost immediately after quitting port—they get drunk. Many of the sailors are said to come on board "half-seas over," and could the skilfullest of pilots save a ship with a drunken crew ?

Be that as it may, the fact remains, that throughout winter almost every week's chronicle at the Lizard is the same story—wild storms, or dense fogs, guns of distress heard, a hasty manning of the life-boat, dragged with difficulty down the steep cliff-road, a brief struggle with the awful sea, and then, even if a few lives are saved, with the ship herself all is over.

"Only last Christmas I saw a vessel go to pieces in ten minutes on the rocks below there," said the man, after particularising several wrecks, which seemed to have imprinted themselves on his memory with all their incidents. "Yes, we have a bad time in winter, and the coastguard men lead a risky life. They are the picked men of the service, and tolerably well paid, but no money could ever pay them for what they go through—or the fishermen, who generally are volunteers, and get little or nothing."

"It must be a hard life in these parts, especially in winter," we observed.

"Well, perhaps it is, but it's our business, you see."

Yes, but not all people do their business, as the mismanagements and mistakes of this world plainly show.

Still, it is a good world, and we felt it so as we strolled along the sunshiny cliff, talking over all these stories, tragical or heroic, which had been told us in such a simple matter-of-fact way, as if they were every-day

M

occurrences. And then, while the young folks went on "for a good scramble" over Penolver, I sat down for a quiet "think"; that enforced rest, which, as years advance, becomes not painful, but actually pleasant; in which, if one fails to solve the problems of the universe, one is prone to con them over, wondering at them all.

From the sunny sea and sunny sky, full of a silence so complete that I could hear every wave as it broke on the unseen rocks below, my mind wandered to that young fellow among his machinery, with his sickly eager face and his short cough—indicating that *his* "business" in this world, over which he seemed so engrossed, might only too soon come to an end. Between these apparently eternal powers of Nature, so strong, so fierce, so irresistible, against which man fought so magnificently with all his perfection of scientific knowledge and accuracy of handiwork—and this poor frail human life, which in a moment might be, blown out like a candle, suddenly quenched in darkness, "there is no skill or knowledge in the grave whither thou goest"—what a contrast it was!

And yet—and yet?—We shall sleep with our fathers, and some of us feel sometimes so tired that we do not in the least mind going to sleep. But notwithstanding this, notwithstanding everything without that seems to imply our perishableness, we are conscious of something within which is absolutely imperishable. We feel it only stronger and clearer as life begins to melt away from us; as "the lights in the windows are darkened, and the daughters of music are brought low." To the young, death is often a terror, for it seems to put an end to the full, rich, passionate life beyond which they can see nothing; but to the old, conscious that this their tabernacle is being slowly dissolved, and yet its mysterious inhabitant, the wonderful, incomprehensible *me*, is exactly the same—thinks, loves, suffers, and enjoys, precisely as it did heaven knows how many years ago—to them, death appears in quite another shape. He is no longer Death the Enemy, but Death the Friend, who may—who can tell?—give back all that life has denied or taken away. He cannot harm us, and he may bless us, with the blessing of loving children, who believe that, whatever happens, nothing can take them out of their Father's arms.

But I had not come to Cornwall to preach, except to myself now and then, as this day. My silent sermon was all done by the time the young folks came back, full of the beauties of their cliff walk, and their affectionate regrets that I "could never manage it," but must have felt so dull, sitting on a stone and watching the sheep and the sea-gulls. Not at all! I was

ENYS DODNAN AND PARDENICK POINTS.

obliged to confess that I never am "dull," as people call it, and love solitude almost as much as society.

M 2

So, each contented in our own way, we went merrily home, to find waiting for us our cosy tea—the last!—and our faithful Charles, who, according to agreement, appeared overnight, to take charge of us till we got back to civilisation and railways.

"Yes, ladies, here I am," said he with a beaming countenance. "And I've got you the same carriage and the same horse, as you wished, and I've come in time to give him a good night's rest. Now, when shall you start, and what do you want to do to-morrow?"

Our idea had been to take for our next resting-place Marazion. This queer-named town had attracted us ever since the days when we learnt geography. Since, we had heard a good deal about it: how it had been inhabited by Jewish colonists, who bought tin from the early Phœnician workers of the Cornish mines, and been called by them Mara-Zion—bitter Zion—corrupted by the common people into Market-Jew. It was a quiet place, with St. Michael's Mount opposite; and attracted us much more than genteel Penzance. So did a letter we got from the landlord of its one hotel, promising to take us in, and make us thoroughly comfortable.

Could we get there in one day? Charles declared we could, and even see a good deal on the road.

"We'll go round by Mullion. Mary will be delighted to get another peep at you ladies, and while I rest the horse you can go in and look at the old church—it's very curious, they say. And then we'll go on to Gunwalloe,—there's another church there, close by the sea, built by somebody who was shipwrecked. But then it's so old and so small. However, we can stop and look at it if you like."

His good common sense, and kindliness, when he might so easily have done his mere duty and taken us the shortest and ugliest route, showing us nothing, decided us to leave all in Charles's hands, and start at 10 A.M. for Penzance, _via_ Helstone, where we all wished to stay an hour or two, and find out a "friend," the only one we had in Cornwall.

So all was settled, with but a single regret, that several boating excursions we had planned with John Curgenven had all fallen through, and we should never behold some wonderful sea-caves between the Lizard and Cadgwith, which we had set our hearts upon visiting.

Charles fingered his cap with a thoughtful air. "I don't see why you shouldn't, ladies. If I was to go direct and tell John Curgenven to have a boat ready at Church Cove, and we was to start at nine instead of ten, and drive there. the carriage might wait while you rowed to the caves and back ; we should still reach Helstone by dinner-time, and Marazion before dark."

"We'll do it!" was the unanimous resolve.   And at this addition to his work Charles looked actually pleased !

So—all was soon over, our easy packing done, our bill paid—a very small one—our goodnights said to the kindly handmaid, Esther, who hoped we would come back again some time, and promised to keep the artistic mural decorations of our little parlour in memory of us.   My young folks went to bed, and then, a little before midnight, when all the house was quiet, I put a shawl over my head, unlatched the innocent door—no bolts or bars at the Lizard—and went out into the night.

What a night it was !—mild as summer, clear as day : the full moon sailing aloft in an absolutely cloudless sky.   Not a breath, not a sound— except the faint thud-thud of the in-coming waves, two miles off, at Kynance, the outline of which, and of the whole coast, was distinctly visible.   A silent earth, lying under a silent heaven.   Looking up, one felt almost like a disembodied soul, free to cleave through infinite space and gain—what ?

Is it human or divine, this ceaseless longing after something never attained, this craving after the eternal life, which, if fully believed in, fully understood, would take all the bitterness out of this life ?   And yet, that knowledge is not given.

But so much is given, and all given is so infinitely good, except where we ourselves turn it into evil, that surely more, and better, will be given to us by and by.

And so, to bed—to bed !   Those only truly enjoy life who fear not death : who can say of the grave as if it were their bed : " I will lay me down in peace and take my rest, for it is Thou only, O God, who makest me to dwell in safety."

DAY THE NINTH

AND our last at the Lizard, which a week ago had been to us a mere word or dot in a map; now we carried away from it a living human interest in everything and everybody.

Esther bade us a cordial farewell: Mrs. Curgenven, standing at the door of her serpentine shop, repeated the good wishes, and informed us that John and his boat had already started for Church Cove. As we drove through the bright little Lizard Town, and past the Church of Landewednack, wondering if we should ever see either again, we felt quite sad.

But sentimental considerations soon vanished in practical alarms. Leaving the carriage and Charles at the nearest point to the Cove, we went down the steep descent, and saw John rocking in his boat, and beckoning to us with a bland and smiling countenance. But between us and him lay a sort of causeway, of the very roughest rocks, slippery with sea-weed, and beat upon by waves—such waves! Yet clearly, if we meant to get into the boat at all, we must seize our opportunity and jump in between the flux and reflux of that advancing tide.

I am not a coward: I love boats, and was well used to them in my youth, but now—my heart misgave me. There were but two alternatives—to stop the pleasure of the whole party, and leave Cornwall with these wonderful sea-caves unseen, or to let my children go alone. Neither was possible; so I hailed a sturdy youth at work hard by, and asked him if he would take charge of an old lady across the rocks. He grinned from ear to ear, but came forward, and did his duty manfully and kindly. My young folks, light as feathers,

JOHN CURGENVEN FISHING.

bounded after; and with the help of John Curgenven, chivalrous and careful as ever, we soon found ourselves safely in the boat.

Safe, but not quite happy. "Here we go up, up, up, and here we go down, down, down," was the principle of our voyage, the most serious one we ever took in an open boat with a single pair of oars. Never did I see such waves,—at least, never did I float upon them, in a boat that went tossing like a bit of cork out into the open sea.

John seemed not to mind them in the least. His strong arms swept the boat along, and he still found breath to talk to us, pointing out the great gloomy cliffs we were passing under, and telling us stories of wrecks, the favourite theme—and no wonder.

This sunshiny morning that iron-bound coast looked awful enough; what must it have looked like, on the winter night when the emigrant ship *Brest* went down!

"Yes, it was about ten o'clock at night," said John. "I was fast asleep in bed, but they knocked me up; I got on my clothes and was off in five minutes. They are always glad enough to get us fishermen, the coastguard are. Mine was the first boat-load we brought ashore; we would only take women and children that time. They were all in their night-gowns, and they couldn't speak a word of English, but we made them understand somehow. One woman threw her three children down to me, and stayed behind on the wreck with two more."

"Were the women frightened?"

"Oh, no, they were very quiet, dazed like. Some of them seemed to be saying their prayers. But they made no fuss at all, not even the little ones. They lay down in the bottom of the boat, and we rowed ashore as fast as we could, to Cadgwith. Then we rowed back and fetched two boat-loads more. We saved a lot of lives that wreck, but only their lives; they had scarcely a rag of clothes on, and some of the babies were as naked as when they were born."

"And who took them in?"

"Everybody: we always do it," answered John, as if surprised at the question. "The fishermen's cottages were full, and so was the parsonage. We gave them clothes, and kept them till they could be sent away. Yes, it was an awful night; I got something to remember it by, here."

He held out his hand, from which we noticed half of one finger was missing.

N

"It got squeezed off with a rope somehow. I didn't heed it much at the time," said John carelessly. "But look, we're at the first of the caves. I'll row in close, ladies, and let you see it."

So we had to turn our minds from the vision of the wreck of the *Brest*, which John's simple words made so terribly vivid, to examine Raven's Ugo, and Dolor Ugo; *ugo* is Cornish for cave. Over the entrance of the first a pair of ravens have built from time immemorial. It is just accessible, the opening being above the sea-line, and hung with quantities of sea-ferns. Here in smuggling days, many kegs of spirits used to be secreted: and many a wild drama no doubt has been acted there—daring encounters between smugglers and coastguard men, not bloodless on either side.

Dolor Ugo is now inaccessible and unusable. Its only floor is of heaving water, a deep olive green, and so clear that we could see the fishes swimming about pursuing a shoal of launce. Its high-vaulted roof and sides were tinted all colours—rose-pink, rich dark brown, and purple. The entrance was wide enough to admit a boat, but it gradually narrowed into impenetrable darkness. How far inland it goes no one can tell, as it could only be investigated by swimming, a rather dangerous experiment. Boats venture as far as the daylight goes; and it is a favourite trick of the boatman suddenly to fire off a pistol, which reverberates like thunder through the mysterious gloom of the cave.

A solemn place; an awful place, some of us thought, as we rowed in, and out again, into the sunshiny open sea. Which we had now got used to; and it was delicious to go dancing like a feather up and down, trusting to John Curgenven's stout arm and fearless, honest face. We felt sad to think this would be our last sight of him and of the magnificent Lizard coast. But the minutes were lessening, and we had some way still to row. Also to land, which meant a leap between the waves upon slippery sea-weedy rocks. In silent dread I watched my children accomplish this feat, and then—

Well, it is over, and I sit here writing these details. But I would not do it again, not even for the pleasure of revisiting Dolor Ugo and having a row with John Curgenven.

Honest fellow! he looked relieved when he saw "the old lady" safe on *terra firma*, and we left him waving adieux, as he "rocked in his boat in the bay." May his stout arms and kindly heart long remain to him! May his summer tourists be many and his winter shipwrecks few! I am sure he will always do his duty, and see that other people do theirs, or, like the proverbial Cornishmen, he "will know the reason why."

Charles was ready; waiting patiently in front of a blacksmith's shop. But, alas! fate had overtaken us in the shape of an innocent leak in John Curgenven's boat; nothing, doubtless, to him, who was in the habit of baling it out with his boots, and then calmly putting them on again, but a little inconvenient to us. To drive thirty miles with one's garments soaked up to the knees was not desirable.

There was a cottage close by, whence came the gleam of a delicious fire and the odour of ironing clothes. We went in: the mistress, evidently a laundress, advanced and offered to dry us—which she did, chattering all the while in the confidential manner of country folks.

A hard working, decent body she was, and as for her house, it was a perfect picture of cleanliness and tidiness. Its two rooms, kitchen and bedroom, were absolutely speckless. When we noticed this, and said we found the same in many Cornish cottages; she almost seemed offended at the praise.

"Oh, that's nothing, ma'am. We hereabouts all likes to have our places tidy. Mine's not over tidy to-day because of the washing. I hadn't time to clean up. But if you was to come of a Sunday. Look there!" Her eye caught something in a dark corner, at which she flew, apron in hand. "I declare, I'm quite ashamed. I didn't think we had one in the house."

"One what?"

"One spider web!"

Dried, warmed, and refreshed, but having found the greatest difficulty in inducing the good woman to receive any tangible thanks for her kindness, we proceeded on our journey; going over the same ground which we had traversed already, and finding Pradenack Down as bleak and beautiful as ever. Our first halt was at the door of Mary Mundy, who, with her unappreciated brother, ran out to meet us, and looked much disappointed when she found we had not come to stay.

"But you will come some time, ladies, and I'll make you so comfortable. And you'll give my duty to the professor"—it was vain to explain that four hundred miles lay between our home and his. "I hope he's quite well.

He was a very nice gentleman, please'm. I shall be delighted to see him again, please'm," &c., &c.

We left the three—Mary, her brother, and Charles—chattering together in a dialect which I do not attempt to reproduce, and sometimes could hardly understand. Us, the natives indulged with their best English, but among themselves they talked the broadest Cornish.

It was a very old church, and a preternaturally old beadle showed it in a passive manner, not recognising in the least its points of interest and beauty, except some rows of open benches with ancient oak backs, wonderfully carved.

"Our vicar dug them up from under the flooring and turned them into pews, There was a gentleman here the other day who said there was nothing like them in all England."

Most curious, in truth, they were, and suited well the fine old building —a specimen of how carefully and lavishly our forefathers built "for God." We, who build for ourselves, are rather surprised to find in out-of-the-way nooks like this, churches that in size and adornment must have cost years upon years of loving labour as well as money.

It was pleasant to know that the present incumbent, a man of archæological tastes, appreciated his blessings, and took the utmost care of his beautiful old church. Success to him! even though he cannot boast the power of his predecessor, the Reverend Thomas Flavel, who died in 1682, and whose monument in the chancel really expresses the sentiments— in epitaph—of the period :

> " Earth, take thine earth ; my sin, let Satan have it ;
> The world my goods ; my soul my God who gave it.
> For from these four, Earth, Satan, World, and God,
> My flesh, my sin, my goods, my soul, I had."

But it does not mention that the reverend gentleman was the best *ghost-layer* in all England, and that when he died his ghost also required to be laid, by a brother clergyman, in a spot on the down still pointed out by the people of Mullion, who, being noted for extreme longevity, have passed down this tradition from generation to generation, with an earnest credulity that we of more enlightened counties can hardly understand.

From Mullion we went on to Gunwalloe. Its church, "small and old," as Charles had depreciatingly said, had been so painfully " restored," and looked so bran-new and uninteresting that we contented ourselves with a distant look. It was close to the sea—probably built on the very spot where its pious founder had been cast ashore. The one curious point about it was the detached belfry, some yards distant from the church itself. It sat alone in a little cove, down which a sluggish river crawled quietly seaward. A sweet quiet place, but haunted, as usual, by tales of cruel shipwrecks—of sailors huddled for hours on a bit of rock just above the waves, till a boat could put out and save the few survivors; of sea treasures continually washed ashore from lost ships—Indian corn, coffee, timber, dollars—many are still found in the sand after a storm. And one treasure more, of which the recollection is still kept at Gunwalloe, "a little dead baby in its cap and night-gown, with a necklace of coral beads."

After this our road turned inland. Our good horse, with the dogged persistency of Cornish horses and Cornish men, plodded on mile after mile. Sometimes for an hour or more we did not meet a living soul; then we came upon a stray labourer, or passed through a village where healthy-looking children, big-eyed, brown-faced, and dirty-handed, picturesque if not pretty, stared at us from cottage doors, or from the gates of cottage gardens full of flowers and apples.

Those apples! They were a picture. Hungry and thirsty, we could not resist them. After passing several trees, hung thickly with delicious fruit, we attacked the owner of one of them, a comely young woman, with a baby in her arms and another at her gown.

"Oh yes, ma'am, you may have as many apples as you like, if your young ladies will go and get them."

And while they did it, she stood talking by the carriage door, pouring out to me her whole domestic history with a simple frankness worthy of the golden age.

"No, really I couldn't," putting back my payment—little enough—for the splendid basket of apples which the girls brought back in triumph. "This is such a good apple year; the pigs would get them if the young ladies didn't. You're kindly welcome to them—well then, if you are determined, say sixpence."

On which magnificent "sixpenn'orth," we lived for days! Indeed I think we brought some of it home as a specimen of Cornish fruit and Cornish liberality.

Helstone was reached at last, and we were not sorry for rest and
food in the old-fashioned inn, whence we could look out of window, and

THE ARMED KNIGHT AND THE LONG SHIP'S LIGHTHOUSE.

contemplate the humours of the little town, which doubtless considered itself
a very great one.   It was market day, and the narrow street was thronged

with beasts and men—the latter as sober as the former, which spoke well for Cornwall. Sober and civil too was every one we addressed in asking our way to the house of our unknown friend, whose only address we had was Helstone. But he seemed well known in the town, though neither a rich man, nor a great man, nor—No, I cannot say he was not a clever man, for in his own line, mechanical engineering, he must have been exceedingly clever. And he was what people call "a great character;" would have made such an admirable study for a novelist, manipulated into an unrecognisable ideal—the only way in which it is fair to put people in books. When I saw him I almost regretted that I write novels no more.

We passed through the little garden—all ablaze with autumn colour, every inch utilised for either flowers, vegetables, or fruit—went into the parlour, sent our cards and waited the result.

In two minutes our friend appeared, and gave us such a welcome! But to explain it I must trench a little upon the sanctities of private life, and tell the story of this honest Cornishman. It will not harm him.

When still young he went to Brazil, and was employed by an English gold-mining company there, for some years. Afterwards he joined an engineering firm, and superintended dredging, the erection of saw-mills, &c., finally building a lighthouse, of which latter work he had the sole charge, and was exceedingly proud. His conscientiousness, probity, and entire reliableness made him most valuable to the firm ; whom he served faithfully for many years. When they, as well as himself, returned to England, he still kept up a correspondence with them, preserving towards every member of the family the most enthusiastic regard and devotion.

He rushed into the parlour, a tall, gaunt, middle-aged man, with a shrewd, kindly face, which beamed all over with delight, as he began shaking hands indiscriminately, saying how kind it was of us to come, and how welcome we were.

It was explained which of us he had specially to welcome, the others being only humble appendages, friends of the family, this well-beloved family, whose likenesses for two generations we saw everywhere about the room.

"Yes, miss, there they all are, your dear grandfather" (alas, only a likeness now!), "your father, and your uncle They were all so good to

me, and I would do anything for them, or for any one of their name. If I
got a message that they wanted me for anything, I'd be off to London, or
to Brazil, or anywhere, in half-an-hour."

And he really looked as if he would.

"But what will you take?" added the good man when the rapture and
excitement of the moment had a little subsided, and his various questions as
to the well-being of "the family" had been asked and answered. "You
have dined, you say, but you'll have a cup of tea. My wife (that's the
little maid I used to talk to your father about, miss; I always told
him I wouldn't stay in Brazil, I must go back to England and marry
my little maid), my wife makes the best cup of tea in all Cornwall.
Here she is!"

And there entered, in afternoon gown and cap, probably just put
on, a middle-aged, but still comely matron, who insisted that, even at
this early hour—3 P.M.—to get a cup of tea for us was "no trouble
at all."

"Indeed, she wouldn't think anything a trouble, no more than
I should, miss, if it was for your family. They never forget me, nor
I them."

It was here suggested that they were not a "forgetting" family. Nor
was he a man likely to be soon forgotten. While the cup of tea, which
proved to be a most sumptuous meal, was preparing, he took us all over his
house, which was full of foreign curiosities, and experimental inventions.
One, I remember, being a musical instrument, a sort of organ, which he had
begun making when a mere boy, and taken with him all the way to Brazil
and back. It had now found refuge in the little room he called his "work-
shop," which was filled with odds and ends that would have been delightful
to a mechanical mind. He expounded them with enthusiasm, and we tried
not to betray an ignorance, which in some of us would have been a sort of
hereditary degradation.

"Ah! they were clever—your father and your uncle!— and how
proud we all were when we finished our light house, and got the Emperor
to light it up for the first time. Look here, ladies, what do you think
this is?"

He took out a small parcel, and solemnly unwrapped from it fold after
fold of paper, till he came to the heart of it—a small wax candle!

"This was the candle the Emperor used to light our lighthouse. I've kept it for nearly thirty years, and I'll keep it as long as I live. Every year on the anniversary of the day I light it, drink his Majesty's health, and the health of all your family, miss, and then I put it out again. So"— carefully re-wrapping the relic in its numerous envelopes—"so I hope it will last my time."

Here the mistress came behind her good man, and they exchanged a smile—the affectionate smile of two who had never been more than two, Darby and Joan, but all sufficient to each other. She announced that tea was ready. And such a tea! How we got through it I hardly know, but travelling is hungry work, and the viands were delicious. The beneficence of our kind hosts, however, was not nearly done.

"Come, ladies, I'll show you my garden, and—(give me a basket and the grape-scissors,)" added he in a conjugal aside. Which resulted in our carrying away with us the biggest bunches in the whole vinery, as well as a quantity of rosy apples, stuffed into every available pocket and bag.

"Nonsense, nonsense," was the answer to vain remonstrances. "D'ye think I wouldn't give the best of everything I had to your family? and so would my missis too. How your father used to laugh at me about my little maid! But he understood it for all that. Oh yes, I'm glad I came home. And now your father and your uncle are home too, and perhaps some day they'll come to see me down here—wouldn't it be a proud day for me! You'll tell them so?"

It was touching, and rare as touching, this passionate personal fidelity. It threw us back, at least such of us as were sentimentally inclined, upon that something in Cornish nature which found its exposition in Arthur and his faithful knights, down to "bold Sir Bedevere," and apparently, is still not lost in Cornwall.

With a sense of real regret, feeling that it would be long ere we might meet his like—such shrewd simplicity, earnest enthusiasm, and exceeding faithfulness—we bade good-bye to the honest man; leaving him and his wife standing at their garden-gate, an elderly Adam and Eve, desiring nothing outside their own little paradise. Which of us could say more, or as much?

Gratefully we "talked them over," as we drove on through the pretty country round Helstone—inland country; for we had no time to go and

o

see the Loe Pool, a small lake, divided from the sea by a bar of sand. This is supposed to be the work of the Cornwall man-demon, Tregeagle; and periodically cut through, with solemn ceremonial, by the Mayor of Helstone, when the "meeting of the waters," fresh and salt, is said to be an extremely curious sight. But we did not see it, nor yet Nonsloe House, close by, which is held by the tenure of having to provide a boat and nets whenever the Prince of Wales or the Duke of Cornwall wishes to fish in the Loe Pool. A circumstance which has never happened yet, certainly!

Other curiosities *en route* we also missed, the stones of Tremenkeverne, half a ton each, used as missiles in a notable fight between two saints, St. Just of the Land's End, and St. Keverne of the Lizard, and still lying in a field to prove the verity of the legend. Also the rock of Goldsithney, where, when the "fair land of Lyonesse" was engulfed by the sea, an ancestor of the Trevelyans saved himself by swimming his horse, and landing; and various other remarkable places, with legends attached, needing much credulity, or imagination, to believe in.

But, fearing to be benighted ere reaching Marazion, we passed them all, and saw nothing more interesting than the ruins of disused tin mines, which Charles showed us, mournfully explaining how the mining business had of late years drifted away from Cornwall, and how hundreds of the once thriving community had been compelled to emigrate or starve. As we neared Marazion, these melancholy wrecks with their little hillocks of mining debris rose up against the evening sky, the image of desolation. And then St. Michael's Mount, the picture in little of Mont St. Michel, in Normandy, appeared in the middle of Mounts' Bay. Lastly, after a gorgeous sunset, in a golden twilight and silvery moonlight, we entered Marazion;—and found it, despite its picturesque name, the most commonplace little town imaginable!

We should have regretted our rash decision, and gone on to Penzance, but for the hearty welcome given us at a most comfortable and home-like inn, which determined us to keep to our first intention, and stay.

So, after our habit of making the best of things, we walked down to the ugly beach, and investigated the dirty-looking bay—in the lowest of all low tides, with a soppy, sea-weedy causeway running across to St. Michael's Mount. By advice of Charles, we made acquaintance with an old boatman he knew, a Norwegian who had drifted hither—shipwrecked, I believe—settled down and married an English woman, but whose English was still of the feeblest kind. However, he had an honest face; so we engaged him to take us out bathing early to-morrow.

"And to-night, ladies?" suggested the faithful Charles. "Wouldn't you like to row round the Mount?—When you've had your tea, I'll come back for you, and help you down to the shore—it's rather rough, but nothing like what you have done, ma'am," added he encouragingly. "And it will be bright moonlight, and the Mount will look so fine."

So, the spirit of adventure conquering our weariness, we went. When I think how it looked next morning—the small, shallow bay, with its toy-castle in the centre, I am glad our first vision of it was under the glamour of moonlight, with the battlemented rock throwing dark shadows across the shimmering sea. In the mysterious beauty of that night row round the Mount, we could imagine anything; its earliest inhabitant, the giant Cormoran, killed by that "valiant Cornishman," the illustrious Jack; the lovely St. Keyne, a king's daughter, who came thither on pilgrimage; and, passing down from legend to history, Henry de la Pomeroy, who, being taken prisoner, caused himself to be bled to death in the Castle; Sir John Arundel, slain on the sands, and buried in the Chapel; Perkin Warbeck's unfortunate wife, who took refuge at St. Michael's shrine, but was dragged thence. And so on, and so on, through the centuries, to the family of St. Aubyn, who bought it in 1660, and have inhabited it ever since. "Very nice people," we heard they were; who have received here the Queen, the Prince of Wales, and other royal personages. What a contrast to the legendary Cormoran!

Yet, looking up as we rowed under the gloomy rock, we could fancy his giant ghost sitting there, on the spot where he killed his wife, for bringing in her apron greenstone, instead of granite, to build the chapel with. Which being really built of greenstone the story must be true! What a pleasure it is to be able to believe anything!

Some of us could have stayed out half the night, floating along in the mild soft air and dreamy moonlight, which made even the commonplace little town look like a fairy scene, and exalted St. Michael's Mount into a grand fortress, fit for its centuries of legendary lore—but others preferred going to bed.

So we landed, and retired. Not however without taking a long look out of the window upon the bay, which now, at high tide, was one sheet of rippling moon-lit water, with the grim old Mount, full of glimmering lights like eyes, sitting silent in the midst of the silent sea.

CORNISH FISHERMAN.

DAY THE TENTH

CANNOT advise Marazion as a bathing place. What a down-come from the picturesque vision of last night, to a small ugly fishy-smelling beach, which seemed to form a part of the town and its business, and was overlooked from everywhere! Yet on it two or three family groups were evidently preparing for a dip, or rather a wade of about a quarter of a mile in exceedingly dirty sea water.

"This will never do," we said to our old Norwegian. "You must row us to some quiet cove along the shore, and away from the town."

He nodded his head, solemn and mute as the dumb boatman of dead Elaine, rowed us out seaward for about half-a-mile, and then proceeded to fasten the boat to a big stone, and walk ashore. The water still did not come much above his knees—he seemed quite indifferent to it. But we?

Well, we could but do at Rome as the Romans do. Toilette in an open boat was evidently the custom of the country. And the sun was warm, the sea safe and shallow. Indeed, so rapidly did it subside, that by the time the bath was done, we were aground, and had to call at the top of our voices to our old man, who sat, with his back to us, dim in the distance, on another big stone, calmly smoking the pipe of peace.

"We'll not try this again," was the unanimous resolve, as, after politely declining a suggestion that "the ladies should walk ashore—" did he think we were amphibious?—we got ourselves floated off at last, and rowed to the nearest landing point, the entrance to St. Michael's Mount.

Probably nowhere in England is found the like of this place. Such a curious mingling of a mediæval fortress and modern residence; of antiquarian treasures and everyday business; for at the foot of the rock is a fishing village of about thirty cottages, which carries on a thriving trade ; and here also is a sort of station for the tiny underground-railway, which worked by a continuous chain, fulfils the very necessary purpose (failing Giant Cormoran, and wife) of carrying up coals, provisions, luggage, and all other domestic necessaries to the hill top.

Thither we climbed by a good many weary steps, and thought, delightful as it may be to dwell on the top of a rock in the midst of the sea, like eagles in an eyrie, there are certain advantages in living on a level country road, or even in a town street. How in the world do the St. Aubyns manage when they go out to dinner ? Two years afterwards, when I read in the paper that one of the daughters of the house, leaning over the battlements, had lost her balance and fallen down, mercifully unhurt, to the rocky slope below—the very spot where we to-day sat so quietly gazing out on the lovely sea view—I felt with a shudder that on the whole, it would be a trying thing to bring up a young family on St. Michael's Mount.

Still, generation after generation of honourable St. Aubyns have brought up their families there, and oh ! what a beautiful spot it is ! How fresh, and yet mild blew the soft sea-wind outside of it, and inside, what endless treasures there were for the archæological mind ! The chapel alone was worth a morning's study, even though shown—odd anachronism—by a footman in livery, who pointed out with great gusto the entrance to a vault discovered during the last repairs, where was found the skeleton of a large man—his bones only—no clue whatever as to who he was or when imprisoned there. The "Jeames" of modern days told us this tale with a noble indifference. Nothing of the kind was likely to happen to him.

Further still we were fortunate enough to penetrate, and saw the Chevy Chase Hall, with its cornice of hunting scenes, the drawing-room, the school-room—only fancy learning lessons there, amidst the veritable evidence of the history one was studying ! And perhaps the prettiest bit of it all was our young guide, herself a St. Aubyn, with her simple grace and sweet courtesy, worthy of one of the fair ladies worshipped by King Arthur's knights.

We did not like encroaching on her kindness, though we could have stayed all day, admiring the curious things she showed us. So we descended the rock, and crossed the causeway, now dry, but very rough walking— certainly St. Michael's Mount has its difficulties as a modern dwelling-house

THE SEINE BOAT—A PERILOUS MOMENT.

—and went back to our inn. For, having given our horse a forenoon's rest, we planned a visit to that spot immortalised by nursery rhyme—

"As I was going to St. Ives
I met a man with seven wives.
Each wife had seven sacks;
Each sack had seven cats;
Each cat had seven kits;
Kits, cats, sacks, and wives,—
How many were there going to St. Ives?"

—One; and after we had been there, we felt sure he never went again!

There were two roads, we learnt, to that immortal town; one very good, but dull; the other bad—and beautiful. We chose the latter, and never repented.

Nor, in passing through Penzance, did we repent not having taken up our quarters there. It was pretty, but so terribly "genteel," so extremely civilised. Glancing up at the grand hotel, we thought with pleasure of our old-fashioned inn at Marazion, where the benign waiter took quite a fatherly interest in our proceedings, even to giving us for dinner our very own blackberries, gathered yesterday on the road, and politely hindering another guest from helping himself to half a dishful, as "they belonged to the young ladies." Truly, there are better things in life than fashionable hotels.

But the neighbourhood of Penzance is lovely. Shrubs and flowers such as one sees on the shores of the Mediterranean grew and flourished in cottage-gardens, and the forest trees we drove under, whole avenues of them, were very fine; gentlemen's seats appeared here and there, surrounded with the richest vegetation, and commanding lovely views. As the road gradually mounted upwards, we saw, clear as in a panorama, the whole coast from the Lizard Point to the Land's End,—which we should behold to-morrow.

For, hearing that every week-day about a hundred tourists in carriages, carts, and omnibuses, usually flocked thither, we decided that the desire of our lives, the goal of our pilgrimage, should be visited by us on a Sunday. We thought that to drive us thither in solitary Sabbatic peace would be fully as good for Charles's mind and morals as to hang all day idle about Marazion; and he seemed to think so himself. Therefore, in prospect of

P

to-morrow, he dealt very tenderly with his horse to-day, and turned us out to walk up the heaviest hills, of which there were several, between Penzance and Castle-an-Dinas.

"There it is," he said at last, stopping in the midst of a wide moor and pointing to a small building, sharp against the sky. "The carriage can't get further, but you can go on, ladies, and I'll stop and gather some blackberries for you."

For brambles, gorse bushes, and clumps of fading heather, with one or two small stunted trees, were now the only curiosities of this, King Arthur's famed hunting castle, and hunting ground, which spread before us for miles and miles. Passing a small farm-house, we made our way to the building Charles pointed out, standing on the highest ridge of the promontory, whose furthest point is the Land's End. Standing there, we could see—or could have seen but that the afternoon had turned grey and slightly misty—the ocean on both sides. Inland, the view seemed endless. Roughtor and Brown Willy, two Dartmoor hills, are said to be visible sometimes. Nearer, little white dots of houses show the mining districts of Redruth and Camborne.

But here, all was desolate solitude. A single wayfarer, looking like a working man in his Sunday best going to visit friends, but evidently tired, as if he had walked for miles, just glanced at us, and passed on. We stood, all alone, on the very spot where many a time must have stood King Arthur, Queen Guinevere, Sir Launcelot, and the other knights— or the real human beings, whether barbarian or not, who formed the originals of those mythical personages.

All had vanished now. Nothing was left but a common-place little tower, built up of the fragments of the old castle, and a wide, pathless moor, over which the wind sighed, and the mist crept. No memorial whatever of King Arthur, except the tradition—which time and change have been powerless to annihilate—that such a man once existed. The long vitality which the legend keeps proves that he must have been a remarkable man in his day. Romance itself cannot exist without a foundation in reality.

So I preached to my incredulous juniors, who threw overboard King Arthur and took to blackberry-gathering; and to conversation with a most comely Cornishwoman, milking the prettiest of Cornish cows in the lonely farm-yard, which was the only sign of humanity for miles and miles. We admired herself and her cattle; we drank her milk, offering for it the usual payment. But the picturesque milkmaid shook her head and demanded just double what even the dearest of London milk-sellers would have asked for the quantity. Which sum we paid in silence, and I only record the fact here in order to state that spite of our foreboding railway friend at Falmouth, this was the only instance in which we were ever "taken in," or in the smallest degree imposed upon, in Cornwall.

Another hour, slowly driving down the gradual slope of the country, through a mining district much more cheerful than that beyond Marazion. The mines were all apparently in full work, and the mining villages were pretty, tidy, and cosy-looking, even picturesque. Approaching St. Ives the houses had quite a foreign look, but when we descended to the town, its dark, narrow streets, pervaded by a "most ancient and fish-like smell," were anything but attractive.

As was our hotel, where, as a matter of duty, we ordered tea, but doubted if we should enjoy it, and went out again to see what little there seemed to be seen, puzzling our way through the gloomy and not too fragrant streets, till at last in despair we stopped a bland, elderly, Methodist-minister-looking gentleman, and asked him the way to the sea.

He eyed us over. "You're strangers here, ma'am?"

I owned the humbling fact, as the inhabitant of St. Ives must doubtless consider it.

"And is it the pilchard fishery you want to see? It is just beginning. A few pilchards have been seen already. There are the boats, the fishermen are all getting ready. It's a fine sight to see them start. Would you like to come and look at them?"

He had turned back and was walking with us down the street, pointing out everything that occurred to him as noticeable, in the kindest and civilest way. When we apologised for troubling him, and would have parted company, our friend made no attempt to go.

"Oh, I've nothing at all to do, except"—he took out the biggest and most respectable of watches—"except to attend a prayer-meeting at half-past six. I should have time to show you the town; we think it is a very nice little town. I ought to know it; I've lived in it, boy and man for thirty-seven years. But now I have left my business to my sons, and I just go

P 2

about and amuse myself, looking into the shop now and then just for curiosity. You must have seen my old shop, ladies, if you came down that street."

Which he named, and also gave us his own name, which we had seen over the shop door, but I shall not record either. Not that I think the honest man is ever likely to read such "light" literature as this book, or to recall the three wanderers to whom he was so civil and kind, and upon whom he poured out an amount of local and personal facts, which we listened to—as a student of human nature is prone to do—with an amused

ST. IVES.

interest in which the comic verged on the pathetic. How large to each man seems his own little world, and what child-like faith he has in its importance to other people! I shall always recall our friend at St. Ives, with his prayer-meetings, his chapel-goings—I concluded he was a Methodist, a sect very numerous in Cornwall—his delight in his successful shop and well-brought-up sons, who managed it so well, leaving him to enjoy his *otium cum dignitate*—no doubt a municipal dignity, for he showed us the Town Hall with great gusto. Evidently to his honest, simple soul, St. Ives was the heart of the world.

By and by again he pulled out the turnip-like watch. " Just ten minutes to get to my prayer-meeting, and I never like to be late, I have been a punctual man all my life, ma'am," added he, half apologetically, till I suggested that this was probably the cause of his peace and success. Upon which he smiled, lifted his hat with a benign adieu, hoped we had liked St. Ives—we had liked his company at any rate—and with a final pointing across the street, " There's my shop, ladies, if you would care to look at it," trotted away to his prayer-meeting.

I believe the neighbourhood of St. Ives, especially Tregenna, its ancient mansion transformed into an hotel, is exceedingly pretty, but night was falling fast, and we saw nothing. Speedily we despatched a most untempting meal, and hurried Charles's departure, lest we should be benighted, as we nearly were, during the long miles of straight and unlovely road—the good road—between here and Penzance. We had done our duty, we had seen the place, but as, in leaving it behind us, we laughingly repeated the nursery rhyme, we came to the conclusion that the man who was "*going* to St. Ives " was the least fortunate of all those notable individuals.

DAY THE ELEVENTH

HE last thing before retiring, we had glanced out on a gloomy sea, a starless sky, pitch darkness, broken only by those moving lights on St. Michael's Mount, and thought anxiously of the morrow. It would be hard, if after journeying thus far and looking forward to it so many years, the day on which we went to the Land's End should turn out a wet day! Still "hope on, hope ever," as we used to write in our copy-books. Some of us, I think, still go on writing it in empty air, and will do so till the hand is dust.

It was with a feeling almost of solemnity that we woke and looked out on the dawn, grey and misty, but still not wet. To be just on the point of gaining the wish of a life-time, however small, is a fact rare enough to have a certain pathos in it. We slept again, and trusted for the best, which by breakfast-time really came, in flickering sun-gleams, and bits of hopeful blue sky. We wondered for the last time, as we had wondered for half a century, "what the Land's End would be like," and then started, rather thoughtful than merry, to find out the truth of the case.

Glad as we were to have for our expedition this quiet Sunday instead of a tumultuous week day, conscience smote us in driving through Penzance, with the church-bells ringing, and the people streaming along to morning service, all in their Sunday best. Perhaps we might manage to go to afternoon church at Sennen, or St. Sennen's, which we knew by report, as the long-deceased father of a family we were acquainted with had been curate there early in the century, and we had promised faithfully "just to go and look at the old place."

But one can keep Sunday sometimes even outside church-doors. I shall never forget the Sabbatic peace of that day; those lonely and lovely roads, first rich with the big trees and plentiful vegetation about Penzance, then gradually growing barer and barer as we drove along the high promontory which forms the extreme point westward of our island. The way along which so many tourist-laden vehicles pass daily was now all solitary; we scarcely saw a soul, except perhaps a labourer leaning over a gate in his decent Sunday clothes, or two or three children trotting to school or church, with their books under their arms. Unquestionably Cornwall is a respectable, sober-minded county; religious-minded too, whether Methodist, Quaker, or other nonconformist sects, of which there are a good many, or decent, conservative Church of England.

We passed St. Buryan's—a curious old church founded on the place where an Irishwoman, Saint Buriana, is said to have made her hermitage. A few stray cottages comprised the whole village. There was nothing special to see, except to drink in the general atmosphere of peace and sunshine and solitude, till we came to Treryn, the nearest point to the celebrated Logan or rocking-stone.

From childhood we had read about it; the most remarkable specimen in England of those very remarkable stones, whether natural or artificial, who can decide?

> "Which the touch of a finger alone sets moving,
> But all earth's powers cannot shake from their base."

Not quite true, this; since in 1824 a rash and foolish Lieutenant Goldsmith (let his name be gibbeted for ever!) did come with a boat's crew, and by main force remove the Logan a few inches from the point on which it rests. Indignant justice very properly compelled him, at great labour and pains, to put it back again, but it has never rocked properly since.

By Charles's advice we took a guide, a solemn-looking youth, who stalked silently ahead of us along the "hedges," which, as at the Lizard, furnished the regular path across the fields coastwards. Soon the gleaming circle of sea again flashed upon us, from behind a labyrinth of rocks, whence we met a couple of tourists returning.

"You'll find it a pretty stiff climb to the Logan, ladies," said one of them in answer to a question.

And so we should have done, indeed, had not our guide's hand been much readier than his tongue.   I, at least, should never have got even so far as that little rock-nest where I located myself—a somewhat anxious-minded old hen—and watched my chickens climb triumphantly that enormous mass of stone which we understood to be the Logan.

"Now, watch it rock!" they shouted across the dead stillness, the lovely solitude of sky and sea.   And I suppose it did rock, but must honestly confess *I* could not see it stir a single inch.

However, it was a big stone, a very big stone, and the stones around it were equally huge and most picturesquely thrown together.   Also—delightful to my young folks!—they furnished the most adventurous scramble that heart could desire.   I alone felt a certain relief when we were all again on smooth ground, with no legs or arms broken.

The cliff-walk between the Logan and the Land's End is said to be one of the finest in England for coast scenery.   Treryn or Treen Dinas, Pardeneck Point, and Tol Pedn Penwith had been named as places we ought to see, but this was impracticable.   We had to content ourselves with a dull inland road, across a country gradually getting more barren and ugly, till we found ourselves suddenly at what seemed the back-yard of a village public-house, where two or three lounging stable-men came forward to the carriage, and Charles jumped down from his box.

"You can get out now, ladies.   This is the Land's End."

"Oh!"

I forbear to translate the world of meaning implied in that brief exclamation.

"Let us go in and get something.   Perhaps we shall admire the place more when we have ceased to be hungry."

The words of wisdom were listened to; and we spent our first quarter of an hour at the Land's End in attacking a skeleton "remain" of not too daintily-cooked beef, and a cavernous cheese, in a tiny back parlour of the—let me give it its right name—First and Last Inn, of Great Britain.

"We never provide for Sunday," said the waitress, responding to a sympathetic question on the difficulty it must be to get food here.   "It's very seldom any tourists come on a Sunday."

At which we felt altogether humbled; but in a few minutes more our contrition passed into sovereign content.

We went out of doors, upon the narrow green plateau in front of the

house, and then we recognised where we were—standing at the extreme end
of a peninsula, with a long line of rocks running out still further into the
sea.   That "great and wide sea, wherein are moving things innumerable,"
the mysterious sea "kept in the hollow of His hand," who is Infinity, and
looking at which, in the intense solitude and silence, one seems dimly to
guess at what Infinity may be.   Any one who wishes to go to church for
once in the Great Temple which His hands have builded, should spend a
Sunday at the Land's End.

At first, our thought had been, What in the world shall we do here for
two mortal hours !   Now, we wished we had had two whole days.   A
sunset, a sunrise, a star-lit night, what would they not have been in this
grand lonely place—almost as lonely as a ship at sea ?   It would be next
best to finding ourselves in the middle of the Atlantic.

But this bliss could not be ; so we proceeded to make the best of what
we had.   The bright day was darkening, and a soft greyness began to creep
over land and sea.   No, not soft, that is the very last adjective applicable
to the Land's End.   Even on that calm day there was a fresh wind—
there must be always wind—and the air felt sharper and more salt than
any sea-air I ever knew.   Stimulating too, so that one's nerves were strung
to the highest pitch of excitement.   We felt able to do anything, without
fear and without fatigue.   So that when a guide came forward—a regular
man-of-war's-man he looked—we at once resolved to adventure along the
line of rocks, seaward, "out as far as anybody was accustomed to go."

"Ay, ay ; I'll take you, ladies.   That is—the young ladies might go—
but you—" eying me over with his keen sailor's glance, full of honesty and
good humour, "you're pretty well on in years, ma'am."

Laughing, I told him how far on, but that I was able to do a good deal
yet.   He laughed too.

"Oh, I've taken ladies much older than you.   One the other day was
nearly seventy.   So we'll do our best, ma'am.   Come along."

He offered a rugged, brown hand, as firm and steady as a mast, to
hold by, and nothing could exceed the care and kindliness with which he
guided every step of every one of us, along that perilous path, that is,
perilous except for cautious feet and steady heads.

"Take care, young ladies.   If you make one false step, you are done for,"
said our guide, composedly as he pointed to the boiling whirl of waters below.

Q

Still, though a narrow and giddy path, there was a path, and the exploit, though a little risky, was not fool-hardy. We should have been

THE LAND'S END AND THE
LOGAN ROCK.

bitterly sorry not to have done it—not to have stood for one grand ten minutes, where in all our lives we may never stand again, at the farthest point where footing is possible, gazing out upon that magnificent circle of sea which sweeps over the submerged "land of Lyonesse," far, far away, into the wide Atlantic.

There were just two people standing with us, clergymen evidently, and one, the guide told us, was "the parson at St. Sennen." We spoke to him, as people do speak, instinctively, when mutually watching such a scene, and by and by we mentioned the name of the long-dead curate of St. Sennen's.

The "parson" caught instantly at the name.

"Mr. —— ? Oh, yes, my father knew him quite well. He used constantly to walk across from Sennen to our house, and take us children long rambles across the cliffs, with a volume of Southey or Wordsworth under his arm. He was a fine young fellow in those days, I have heard, and an excellent clergyman. And he afterwards married a very nice girl from the north somewhere."

"Yes;" we smiled. The "nice girl" was now a sweet silver-haired little lady of nearly eighty; the "fine young fellow" had long since departed; and the boy was this grave middle-aged gentleman, who remembered both as a tradition of his youth. What a sermon it all preached, beside this eternal rock, this ever-moving, never-changing sea!

But time was passing—how fast it does pass, minutes, ay, and years! We bade adieu to our known unknown friend, and turned our feet backwards, cautiously as ever, stopping at intervals to listen to the gossip of our guide.

"Yes, ladies, that's the spot—you may see the hoof-mark—where General Armstrong's horse fell over; he just slipped off in time, but the poor beast was drowned. And here, over that rock, happened the most curious thing. I wouldn't have believed it myself, only I knew a man that saw it with his own eyes. Once a bullock fell off into the pool below there—just look, ladies." (We did look, into a perfect Maëlstrom of boiling waves.) "Everybody thought he was drowned, till he was seen swimming about unhurt. They fished him up, and exhibited him as a curiosity."

And again, pointing to a rock far out in the sea.

" That's the Brisons. Thirty years ago a ship went to pieces there, and the captain and his wife managed to climb on to that rock. They held on there for two days and a night, before a boat could get at them. At last they were taken off one at a time, with rockets and a rope; the wife first. But the rope slipped and she fell into the water. She was pulled out in a minute or so, and rowed ashore, but they durst not tell her husband she was drowned. I was standing on the beach at Whitesand Bay when the boat came in. I was only a lad, but I remember it well, and her too lifted out all dripping and quite dead. She was such a fine woman."

"And the captain?"

"They went back for him, and got him off safe, telling him nothing. But when he found she was dead he went crazy-like—kept for ever saying, 'She saved my life, she saved my life,' till he was taken away by his friends. Look out, ma'am, mind your footing; just here a lady slipped and broke her leg a week ago. I had to carry her all the way to the hotel. I shouldn't like to carry you."

We all smiled at the comical candour of the honest sailor, who proceeded to give us bits of his autobiography. He was Cornish born, but had seen a deal of the world as an A.B. on board her Majesty's ship *Agamemnon*.

"Of course you have heard of the *Agamemnon*, ma'am. I was in her off Balaklava. You remember the Crimean war?"

Yes, I did. His eyes brightened as we discussed names and places once so familiar, belonging to that time, which now seems so far back as to be almost historical.

"Then you know what a winter we had, and what a summer afterwards. I came home invalided, and didn't attempt the service afterwards; but I never thought I should come home at all. Yes, it's a fine place the Land's End, though the air is so strong that it kills some folks right off. Once an invalid gentleman came, and he was dead in a fortnight. But I'm not dead yet, and I stop here mostly all the year round."

He sniffed the salt air and smiled all over his weather-beaten face—keen, bronzed, blue-eyed, like one of the old Vikings. He was a fine specimen of a true British tar. When, having seen all we could, we gave him his small honorarium, he accepted it gratefully, and insisted on our taking in return a memento of the place in the shape of a stone weighing about two pounds, glittering with ore, and doubtless valuable, but ponderous. Oh, the trouble it gave me to carry it home, and pack and unpack it among my small luggage! But I did bring it home, and I keep it still in remembrance of the Land's End, and of the honest sailor of H.M.S. *Agamemnon*.

So all was over. We could dream of an unknown Land's End no more. It became now a real place, of which the reality, though different from the imagination, was at least no disappointment. How few people in attaining a life-long desire can say as much!

Our only regret, an endurable one now, was that we had not carried out our original plan of staying some days there—tourist-haunted, troubled days they might have been, but the evenings and mornings would have been glorious. With somewhat heavy hearts we summoned Charles and the carriage, for already a misty drift of rain began sweeping over the sea.

"Still, we must see Whitesand Bay," said one of us, recalling a story a friend had once told how, staying at Land's End, she crossed the bay alone in a blinding storm, took refuge at the coastguard station, where she was hospitably received, and piloted back with most chivalric care by a coastguard, who did not tell her till their journey's end that he had left at home a wife, and a baby just an hour old.

No such romantic adventure befell us. We only caught a glimmer of the bay through drizzling rain, which by the time we reached Sennen village had become a regular downpour. Evidently, we could do no more that day, which was fast melting into night.

"We'll go home," was the sad resolve, glad nevertheless that we had a comfortable "home" to go to.

So closing the carriage and protecting ourselves as well as we could from the driving rain, we went forward, passing the Quakers' burial ground, where is said to be one of the finest views in Cornwall; the Nine Maidens, a circle of Druidical stones, and many other interesting things, without once looking at or thinking of them.

Half a mile from Marazion the rain ceased, and a light like that of the rising moon began to break through the clouds. What a night it might be, or might have been, could we have stayed at the Land's End!

That ghostly "might have been!" It is in great things as in small, the worry, the torment, the paralysing burden of life. Away with it! We have done our best to be happy, and we have been happy. We have seen the Land's End.

DAY THE TWELFTH

ONDAY morning. Black Monday we were half inclined to call it, knowing that by the week's end our travels must be over and done, and that if we wished still to see all we had planned, we must inevitably next morning return to civilisation and railways, a determination which involved taking this night "a long, a last farewell" of our comfortable carriage and our faithful Charles.

"But it needn't be until night," said he, evidently loth to part from his ladies. "If I get back to Falmouth' by daylight to-morrow morning, master will be quite satisfied. I can take you wherever you like to-day."

"And the horse?"

"Oh, he shall get a good feed and a rest till the middle of the night, then he'll do well enough. We shall have the old moon after one o'clock to get home by. Between Penzance and Falmouth it's a good road, though rather lonely."

I should think it was, in the "wee hours" by the dim light of a waning moon. But Charles seemed to care nothing about it, so we said no more, but decided to take the drive—our last drive.

Our minds were perplexed between Botallack Mine, the Gurnard's Head, Lamorna Cove, and several other places, which we were told we must on no account miss seeing, the first especially. Some of us, blessed with scientific relatives, almost dreaded returning home without having seen a single Cornish mine ; others, lovers of scenery, longed for more of that magnificent coast. But finally, a meek little voice carried the day.

"I was so disappointed—more than I liked to say—when it rained,

SENNEN COVE. WAITING FOR THE BOATS.

and I couldn't get my shells for our bazaar. How shall I ever get them now? If it wouldn't trouble anybody very much, mightn't we go again to Whitesand Bay?"

A plan not wholly without charm. It was a heavenly day; to spend it in delicious idleness on that wide sweep of sunshiny sand would be a rest for the next day's fatigue. Besides, consolatory thought! there would be no temptation to put on miners' clothes, and go dangling in a basket down to the heart of the earth, as the Princess of Wales was reported to have done. The pursuit of knowledge may be delightful, but some of us owned to a secret preference for *terra firma* and the upper air. We resolved to face opprobrium, and declare boldly we had "no time" (needless to add no inclination) to go and see Botallack Mine. The Gurnard's Head cost us a pang to miss; but then we should catch a second view of the Land's End. Yes, we would go to Whitesand Bay.

It was a far shorter journey in sunshine than in rain, even though we made various divergencies for blackberries and other pleasures. Never had the sky looked bluer or the sea brighter, and much we wished that we could have wandered on in dreamy peace, day after day, or even gone through England, gipsy-fashion, in a house upon wheels, which always seemed to me the very ideal of travelling.

We reached Sennen only too soon. Pretty little Sennen, with its ancient church and its new school house, where the civil schoolmaster gave me some ink to write a post-card for those to whom even the post-mark "Sennen" would have a touching interest, and where the boys and girls, released for dinner, were running about. Board school pupils, no doubt, weighted with an amount of learning which would have been appalling to their grandfathers and grandmothers, the simple parishioners of the "fine young fellow" half a century ago. As we passed through the village with its pretty cottages and "Lodgings to Let," we could not help thinking what a delightful holiday resort this would be for a large small family, who could be turned out as we were when the carriage could no farther go, on the wide sweep of green common, gradually melting into silvery sand, so fine and soft that it was almost a pleasure to tumble down the slopes, and get up again, shaking yourself like a dog, without any sense of dirt or discomfort. What a paradise for children, who might burrow like rabbits and wriggle about like sand-eels, and never come to any harm!

R

Without thought of any danger, we began selecting our bathing-place, shallow enough, with long strips of wet shimmering sand to be crossed before reaching even the tiniest waves; when one of us, the cautious one, appealed to an old woman, the only human being in sight.

"Bathe?" she said. "Folks ne'er bathe here. 'Tain't safe."

"Why not? Quicksands?"

She nodded her head. Whether she understood us or not, or whether we quite understood her, I am not sure, and should be sorry to libel such a splendid bathing ground—apparently. But maternal wisdom interposed, and the girls yielded. When, half an hour afterwards, we saw a solitary figure moving on a distant ledge of rock, and a black dot, doubtless a human head, swimming or bobbing about in the sea beneath—maternal wisdom was reproached as arrant cowardice. But the sand was delicious, the sea-wind so fresh, and the sea so bright, that disappointment could not last. We made an encampment of our various impedimenta, stretched ourselves out, and began the search for shells, in which every arm's-length involved a mine of wealth and beauty.

Never except at one place, on the estuary of the Mersey, have I seen a beach made up of shells so lovely in colour and shape; very minute; some being no bigger than a grain of rice or a pin's head. The collecting of them was a fascination. We forgot all the historical interests that ought to have moved us, saw neither Athelstan, King Stephen, King John, nor Perkin Warbeck, each of whom is said to have landed here— what were they to a tiny shell, like that moralised over by Tennyson in " Maud "—" small, but a work divine"? I think infinite greatness sometimes touches one less than infinite littleness—the exceeding tenderness of Nature, or the Spirit which is behind Nature, who can fashion with equal perfectness a starry hemisphere and a glow-worm; an ocean and a little pink shell. The only imperfection in creation seems—oh, strange mystery!— to be man. Why?

But away with moralising, or dreaming, though this was just a day for dreaming, clear, bright, warm, with not a sound except the murmur of the low waves, running in an enormous length—curling over and breaking on the soft sands. Everything was so heavenly calm, it seemed impossible to believe in that terrible scene when the captain and his wife were seen clinging to the Brisons rock, just ahead.

Doubtless our friend of the *Agamemnon* was telling this and all his other stories to an admiring circle of tourists, for we saw the Land's End covered with a moving swarm like black flies. How thankful we felt that we had "done" it on a Sunday! Still, we were pleased to have another gaze at it, with its line of picturesque rocks, the Armed Knight and the Irish Lady—though, I confess, I never could make out which was the knight and which was the lady. Can it be that some fragment of the legend of Tristram and Iseult originated these names?

After several sweet lazy hours, we went through a "fish-cellar," a little group of cottages, and climbed a headland, to take our veritable farewell of the Land's End, and then decided to go home. We had rolled or thrown our provision basket, rugs, &c., down the sandy slope, but it was another thing to carry them up again. I went in quest of a small boy, and there presented himself a big man, coastguard, as the only unemployed hand in the place, who apologised with such a magnificent air for not having "cleaned" himself, that I almost blushed to ask him to do such a menial service as to carry a bundle of wraps. But he accepted it, conversing amiably as we went, and giving me a most graphic picture of life at Sennen during the winter. When he left me, making a short cut to our encampment—a black dot on the sands, with two moving black dots near it—a fisher wife joined me, and of her own accord began a conversation.

She and I fraternised at once, chiefly on the subject of children, a group of whom were descending the road from Sennen School. She told me how many of them were hers, and what prizes they had gained, and what hard work it was. She could neither read nor write, she said, but she liked her children to be good scholars, and they learnt a deal up at Sennen.

Apparently they did, and something else besides learning, for when I had parted from my loquacious friend, I came up to the group just in time to prevent a stand-up fight between two small mites, the *casus belli* of which I could no more arrive at, than a great many wiser people can discover the origin of national wars. So I thought the strong hand of "intervention" —civilised intervention—was best, and put an end to it, administering first a good scolding, and then a coin. The division of this coin among the little party compelled an extempore sum in arithmetic, which I required them to do (for the excellent reason that I couldn't do it myself!)—and they did it! Therefore I conclude that the heads of the Sennen school-children are as solid as their fists, and equally good for use.

ON THE ROAD TO ST. NIGHTON'S
KEEVE

Simple little com-munity! which as the fisher wife told me, only goes to Penzance about once a year, and is, as yet, innocent of tourists, for the swarm at the Land's End seldom goes near Whitesand Bay. Ex-istence here must be very much that of an oyster,—but perhaps oysters are happy.

By the time we reached Penzance the lovely day was dying into an equally lovely evening. St. Michael's Mount shone in the setting sun. It was high water, the bay was all alive with boats, and there was quite a little crowd of people gathered at the mild little station of Marazion. What could be happening?

A princess was expected, that young half-English, half-foreign princess, in whose romantic story the British public has taken such an interest, sympathising with the motherly kindness of our good Queen, with the wedding at Windsor, and the sad little infant funeral there, a year after. The Princess Frederica of Hanover, and the Baron Von Pawel-Rammingen, her father's secretary, who, like a stout mediæval knight, had loved, wooed, and married her, were coming to St. Michael's Mount on a visit to the St. Aubyns.

Marazion had evidently roused itself, and risen to the occasion. Half the town must have turned out to the beach, and the other half secured every available boat, in which it followed, at respectful distance, the two boats, one full of luggage, the other of human beings, which were supposed to be the royal party. People speculated with earnest curiosity, which was the princess, and which her husband, and what the St. Aubyns would do with them; whether they would be taken to see the Land's End, and whether they would go there as ordinary tourists, or in a grand visit of state. How hard it is that royal folk can never see anything except in state, or in a certain adventitious garb, beautiful, no doubt, but satisfactorily hiding the real thing. How they must long sometimes for a walk, after the fashion of Haroun Alraschid, up and down Regent Street and Oxford Street! or an incognito foreign tour, or even a solitary country walk, without a "lady-in-waiting."

We had no opera-glass to add to the many levelled at those two boats, so we went in—hoping host and guests would spend a pleasant evening in the lovely old rooms we knew. We spent ours in rest, and in arranging for to-morrow's flight. Also in consulting with our kindly landlady as to a possible house at Marazion for some friends whom the winter might drive southwards, like the swallows, to a climate which, in this one little bay shut out from east and north, is—they told us—during all the cruel months which to many of us means only enduring life, not living—as mild and equable almost as the Mediterranean shores. And finally, we settled all with our faithful Charles, who looked quite mournful at parting with his ladies.

"Yes, it is rather a long drive, and pretty lonely," said he. "But I'll wait till the moon's up, and that'll help us. We'll get into Falmouth by daylight. I've got to do the same thing often enough through the summer, so I don't mind it."

Thus said the good fellow, putting a cheery face on it, then with a hasty "Good-bye, ladies," he rushed away. But we had taken his address, not meaning to lose sight of him. (Nor have we done so up to this date of writing; and the fidelity has been equal on both sides.)

Then, in the midst of a peal of bells which was kept up unweariedly till 10 P.M.—evidently Marazion is not blessed with the sight of a princess every day—we closed our eyes upon all outward things, and went away to the Land of Nod.

DAY THE THIRTEENTH

INTO King Arthur's land—Tintagel his birth-place, and Camelford, where he fought his last battle—the legendary region of which one may believe as much or as little as one pleases—we were going to-day. With the good common sense which we flattered ourselves had accompanied every step of our unsentimental journey, we had arranged all before-hand, ordered a carriage to meet the mail train, and hoped to find at Tintagel—not King Uther Pendragon, King Arthur or King Mark, but a highly respectable landlord, who promised us a welcome at an inn—which we only trusted would be as warm and as kindly as that we left behind us at Marazion.

The line of railway which goes to the far west of England is one of the prettiest in the kingdom on a fine day, which we were again blessed with. It had been a wet summer, we heard, throughout Cornwall, but in all our journey, save that one wild storm at the Lizard, sunshine scarcely ever failed us. Now—whether catching glimpses of St. Ives Bay or sweeping through the mining district of Redruth, and the wooded country near Truro, Grampound, and St. Austell, till we again saw the glittering sea on the other side of Cornwall—all was brightness. Then darting inland once more, our iron horse carried us past Lostwithiel, the little town which once boasted Joseph Addison, M.P., as its representative ; gave us a fleeting vision of Ristormel, one of the ancient castles of Cornwall, and on through a leafy land, beginning to change from rich green to the still richer yellows and reds of autumn, till we stopped at Bodmin Road.

No difficulty in finding our carriage, for it was the only one there ; a huge vehicle, of ancient build, the horses to match, capable of accommodating a whole family and its luggage. We missed our compact little machine, and

TINTAGEL.

our brisk, kindly Charles, but soon settled ourselves in dignified, roomy state, for the twenty miles, or rather more, which lay between us and the coast.

Our way ran along lonely quiet country roads and woods almost as green as when Queen Guinevere rode through them "a maying," before the dark days of her sin and King Arthur's death.

Here it occurs to me, as it did this day to a practical youthful mind, "What in the world do people know about King Arthur?"

Well, most people have read Tennyson, and a few are acquainted with the "Morte d'Arthur" of Sir Thomas Malory. But, perhaps I had better briefly give the story, or as much of it as is necessary for the edification of outsiders.

Uther Pendragon, King of Britain, falling in love with Ygrayne, wife of the duke of Cornwall, besieged them in their twin castles of Tintagel and Terrabil, slew the husband, and the same day married the wife. Unto whom a boy was born, and by advice of the enchanter Merlin, carried away, from the sea-shore beneath Tintagel, and confided to a good knight, Sir Ector, to be brought up as his own son, and christened Arthur. On the death of the king, Merlin produced the youth, who was recognized by his mother Ygrayne, and proclaimed king in the stead of Uther Pendragon. He instituted the Order of Knights of the Round Table, who were to go everywhere, punishing vice and rescuing oppressed virtue, for the love of God and of some noble lady. He married Guinevere, daughter of King Leodegrance, who forsook him for the love of Sir Launcelot, his bravest knight and dearest friend. One by one, his best knights fell away into sin, and his nephew Mordred raised a rebellion, fought with him, and conquered him at Camelford. Seeing his end was near, Arthur bade his last faithful knight, Sir Bedevere, carry him to the shore of a mere (supposed to be Dozmare Pool) and throw in there his sword Excalibur; when appeared a boat with three queens, who lifted him in, mourning over him. With them he sailed away across the mere, to be healed of his grievous wound. Some say that he was afterwards buried in a chapel near, others declare that he lives still in fairy land, and will reappear in latter days, to reinstate the Order of Knights of the Round Table, and rule his beloved England, which will then be perfect as he once tried to make it, but in vain.

Camelford of to-day is certainly not the Camelot of King Arthur— but a very respectable, commonplace little town, much like other country towns; the same genteel linendrapers' and un-genteel ironmongers' shops; the same old-established commercial inn, and a few ugly, but solid-looking

S

private houses, with their faces to the street and their backs nestled in gardens and fields. Some of the inhabitants of these said houses were to be seen taking a quiet afternoon stroll. Doubtless they are eminently respectable and worthy folk, leading a mild provincial life like the people in Miss Martineau's *Deerbrook*, or Miss Austin's *Pride and Prejudice*—of which latter quality they have probably a good share.

We let our horses rest, but we ourselves felt not the slightest wish to rest at Camelford, so walked leisurely on till we came to the little river Camel, and to Slaughter Bridge, said to be the point where King Arthur's army was routed and where he received his death-wound. A slab of stone, some little distance up the stream, is still called "King Arthur's Tomb." But as his coffin is preserved, as well as his Round Table, at Winchester; where, according to mediæval tradition, the bodies of both Arthur and Guinevere were found, and the head of Guinevere had yellow hair; also that near the little village of Davidstow, is a long barrow, having in the centre a mound, which is called "King Arthur's grave"—inquiring minds have plenty of "facts" to choose from. Possibly at last they had better resort to fiction, and believe in Arthur's disappearance, as Tennyson makes him say,

"To the island-valley of Avillion. . .
Where I may heal me of my grievous wound."

Dozmare Pool we found so far out of our route that we had to make a virtue of necessity, and imagine it all; the melancholy moorland lake, with the bleak hill above it, and stray glimpses of the sea beyond. A ghostly spot, and full of many ghostly stories besides the legend of Arthur. Here Tregeagle, the great demon of Cornwall, once had his dwelling, until, selling his soul to the devil, his home was sunk to the bottom of the mere, and himself is heard of stormy nights, wailing round it with other ghost-demons, in which the Cornish mind still lingeringly believes. Visionary packs of hounds; a shadowy coach and horses, which drives round and round the pool, and then drives into it; flitting lights, kindled by no human hand, in places where no human foot could go—all these tales are still told by the country folk, and we might have heard them all. Might also have seen, in fancy, the flash of the "brand Excalibur"; heard the wailing song of the three queens; and pictured the dying Arthur lying on the lap of his sister Morgane la Faye. But, I forgot, this is an un-sentimental journey.

The Delabole quarries are as un-sentimental a place as one could desire. It was very curious to come suddenly upon this world of slate, piled up in enormous masses on either side the road, and beyond them hills of debris, centuries old—for the mines have been worked ever since the time of Queen Elizabeth. Houses, walls, gates, fences, everything that can possibly be made of slate, is made. No green or other colour tempers the all-pervading shade of bluish-grey, for vegetation in the immediate vicinity of the quarries is abolished, the result of which would be rather dreary, save for the cheerful atmosphere of wholesome labour, the noise of waggons, horses, steam-engines—such a contrast to the silence of the deserted tin-mines.

But, these Delabole quarries passed, silence and solitude come back again. Even the yearly-increasing influx of tourists fails to make the little village of Trevena anything but a village, where the said tourists lounge about in the one street, if it can be called a street, between the two inns and the often-painted, picturesque old post-office. Everything looked so simple, so home-like, that we were amused to find we had to get ready for a *table d'hôte* dinner, in the only available eating room where the one indefatigable waitress, a comely Cornish girl, who seemed Argus and Briareus rolled into one, served us—a party small enough to make conversation general, and pleasant and intelligent enough to make it very agreeable, which does not always happen at an English hotel.

Then we sallied out to find the lane which leads to Tintagel Castle, or Castles—for one sits in the sea, the other on the opposite heights in the mainland, with power of communicating by the narrow causeway which now at least exists between the rock and the shore. This seems to confirm the legend, how the luckless husband of Ygrayne shut up himself and his wife in two castles, he being slain in the one, and she married to the victorious King Uther Pendragon, in the other.

Both looked so steep and dangerous in the fast-coming twilight that we thought it best to attempt neither, so contented ourselves with a walk on the cliffs and the smooth green field which led thither. Leaning against a gate, we stood and watched one of the grandest out of the many grand sunsets which had blessed us in Cornwall. The black rock of Tintagel filled the foreground ; beyond, the eye saw nothing but sea, the sea which covers vanished Lyonesse, until it met the sky, a clear amber with long bars like waves, so that you could hardly tell where sea ended and

S 2

sky began.   Then into it there swam slowly a long low cloud, shaped like a boat, with a raised prow, and two or three figures sitting at the stern.

"King Arthur and the three queens," we declared, and really a very moderate imagination could have fancied it this.   "But what is that long black thing at the bow?"

"Oh," observed drily the most practical of the three, "it's King Arthur's luggage."

Sentiment could survive no more.   We fell into fits of laughter, and went home to tea and bed.

DAYS FOURTEENTH, FIFTEENTH, AND SIXTEENTH—

AND all Arthurian days, so I will condense them into one chapter, and not spin out the hours that were flying so fast. Yet we hardly wished to stop them; for pleasant as travelling is, the best delight of all is— the coming home.

Walking, to one more of those exquisite autumn days, warm as summer, yet with a tender brightness that hot summer never has, like the love between two old people, out of whom all passion has died—we remembered that we were at Tintagel, the home of Ygrayne and Arthur, of King Mark and Tristram and Iseult. I had to tell that story to my girls in the briefest form, how King Mark sent his nephew, Sir Tristram, to fetch home Iseult of Ireland for his queen, and on the voyage Bragswaine, her handmaiden, gave each a love-potion, which caused the usual fatal result; how at last Tristram fled from Tintagel into Brittany, where he married another Iseult "of the white hands," and lived peacefully, till, stricken by death, his fancy went back to his old love, whom he implored to come to him. She came, and found him dead. A tale—of which the only redeeming point is the innocence, simplicity, and dignity of the second Iseult, the unloved Breton wife, to whom none of our modern poets who have sung or travestied the wild, passionate, miserable, ugly story, have ever done full justice.

These sinful lovers, the much-wronged but brutal King Mark, the scarcely less brutal Uther Pendragon, and hapless Ygrayne—what a curious condition of morals and manners the Arthurian legends unfold! A time when might was right; when every one seized what he wanted just because he wanted it, and kept it, if he could, till a stronger hand wrenched it from him. That in such a state of society there should ever have arisen the dimmest dream of a man like Arthur—not perhaps Tennyson's Arthur, the "blameless king," but even Sir Thomas Malory's, founded on mere tradition—is a remarkable thing. Clear through all the mists of ages shines that ideal of knighthood, enjoining courage, honour, faith, chastity, the worship of God and the service of men. Also, in the very highest degree, inculcating that chivalrous love of woman—not women —which barbaric nations never knew. As we looked at that hoar ruin sitting solitary in the sunny sea, and thought of the days when it was a complete fortress, inclosing a mass of human beings, all with human joys, sorrows, passions, crimes—things that must have existed in essence, however legend has exaggerated or altered them—we could not but feel that the mere possibility of a King Arthur shining down the dim vista of long-past centuries, is something to prove that goodness, like light, has an existence as indestructible as Him from whom it comes.

We looked at Tintagel with its risky rock-path. "It will be a hot climb, and our bathing days are numbered. Let us go in the opposite direction to Bossinney Cove."

Practicality when weighed against Poetry is poor—Poetry always kicks the beam. We went to Bossinney.

Yet what a pretty cove it was! and how pleasant! While waiting for the tide to cover the little strip of sand, we re-mounted the winding path, and settled ourselves like seabirds on the furthermost point of rock, whence, just by extending a hand, we could have dropped anything, ourselves even, into a sheer abyss of boiling waves, dizzy to look down into, and yet delicious.

So was the bath, though a little gloomy, for the sun could barely reach the shut-in cove; and we were interfered with considerably by—not tourists—but a line of donkeys! They were seen solemnly descending the narrow cliff-path one by one—eleven in all—each with an empty sack over his shoulder. Lastly came a very old man, who, without taking the least notice of us, disposed himself to fill these sacks with sand. One after the other the eleven meek animals came forward and submitted each

CRESWICK'S MILL IN THE ROCKY VALLEY.

to his load, which proceeding occupied a good hour and a half. I hardly know which was the most patient, the old man or his donkeys.

We began some of us to talk to his beasts, and others to himself. "Yes, it was hard work," he said, "but he managed to come down to the cove three times a day. And the asses were good asses. They all had their names; Lucy, Cherry, Sammy, Tom, Jack, Ned;" each animal pricked up its long ears and turned round its quiet eyes when called. Some were young and some old, but all were very sure-footed, which was necessary here. "The weight some of 'em would carry was wonderful."

The old man seemed proud of the creatures, and kind to them too in a sort of way. He had been a fisherman, he said, but now was too old for that; so got his living by collecting sand.

"It makes capital garden-paths, this sand. I'd be glad to bring you some, ladies," said he, evidently with an eye to business. When we explained that this was impracticable, unless he would come all the way to London, he merely said, "Oh," and accepted the disappointment. Then bidding us a civil "Good day," he disappeared with his laden train.

Poor old fellow! Nothing of the past knightly days, nothing of the busy existing modern present affected him, or ever would do so. He might have been own brother, or cousin, to Wordsworth's "Leech-gatherer on the lonely moor." Whenever we think of Bossinney Cove, we shall certainly think of that mild old man and his eleven donkeys.

The day was hot, and it had been a steep climb; we decided to drive in the afternoon, "for a rest," to Boscastle.

Artists and tourists haunt this picturesque nook. A village built at the end of a deep narrow creek, which runs far inland, and is a safe shelter for vessels of considerable size. On either side is a high footpath, leading to two headlands, from both of which the views of sea and coast are very fine. And there are relics of antiquity and legends thereto belonging—a green mound, all that remains of Bottrieux Castle; and Ferrabury Church, with its silent tower. A peal of bells had been brought, and the ship which carried them had nearly reached the cove, when the pilot, bidding the captain "thank God for his safe voyage," was answered that he "thanked only himself and a fair wind." Immediately a storm arose; and the ship went down with every soul on board—except the pilot. So the church tower is mute—but on winter

T

nights the lost bells are still heard, sounding mournfully from the depths of the sea.

As we sat, watching with a vague fascination the spouting, minute by minute, of a "blow-hole," almost as fine as the Kynance post-office—we moralised on the story of the bells, and on the strange notions people have, even in these days, of Divine punishments; imputing to the Almighty Father all their own narrow jealousies and petty revenges, dragging down God into the likeness of men, such an one as themselves, instead of .striving to lift man into the image of God.

Meantime the young folks rambled and scrambled—watched with anxious and even envious eyes—for it takes one years to get entirely reconciled to the quiescence of the down-hill journey. And then we drove slowly back—just in time for another grand sunset, with Tintagel black in the foreground, until it and all else melted into darkness, and there was nothing left but to

> "Watch the twilight stars come out
> Above the lonely sea."

Next morning we must climb Tintagel, for it would be our last day.

And what a heavenly day it was! How softly the waves crept in upon the beach—just as they might have done when they laid at Merlin's feet "the little naked child," disowned of man but dear to Heaven, who was to grow up into the "stainless king."

He and his knights—the "shadowy people of the realm of dream,"— were all about us, as, guided by a rheumatic old woman, who climbed feebly up the stair, where generations of ghostly feet must have ascended and descended, we reached a bastion and gateway, quite pre-historic. Other ruins apparently belong to the eleventh or twelfth centuries. But to this there is no clue. It may have been the very landing-place of King Uther or King Mark, or other Cornish heroes, who held this wonderful natural-artificial fortress in the dim days of old romance.

"Here are King Arthur's cups and saucers," said the old woman, pausing in the midst of a long lament over her own ailments, to point out some holes in the slate rock. "And up there you'll find the chapel. It's an easy climb—if you mind the path—just where it passes the spring."

BOSCASTLE.

That spring, trickling down from the very top of the rock, and making a verdant space all round it—what a treasure it must have been to the unknown inhabitants who, centuries ago, entrenched themselves here—for offence or defence—against the main-land. Peacefully it flowed on still, with the little ferns growing, and the sheep nibbling beside it. We idle tourists alone occupied that solitary height where those long-past warlike races—one succeeding the other—lived and loved, fought and died.

The chapel—where the high altar and a little burial-ground beside it can still be traced—is clearly much later than Arthur's time. However, there are so few data to go upon, and the action of sea-storms destroys so much every year, that even to the learned archæologist, Tintagel is a great mystery, out of which the imaginative mind may evolve almost anything it likes.

We sat a long time on the top of the rock—realising only the one obvious fact that our eyes were gazing on precisely the same scene, seawards and coastwards, that all these long-dead eyes were accustomed to behold. Beaten by winds and waves till the grey of its slate formation is nearly black ; worn into holes by the constant action of the tide which widens yearly the space between it and the main-land, and gnaws the rock below into dangerous hollows that in time become sea-caves, Tintagel still remains—and one marvels that so much of it does still remain—a land-mark of the cloudy time between legend and actual history.

Whether the ruin on the opposite height was once a portion of Tintagel Castle, before the sea divided it, making a promontory into an island—or whether it was the Castle Terrabil, in which Gorlois, Ygrayne's husband, was slain—no one now can say. That both the twin fortresses were habitable till Elizabeth's time, there is evidence to prove. But since then they have been left to decay, to the silent sheep and the screeching ravens, including doubtless that ghostly chough, in whose shape the soul of King Arthur is believed still to revisit the familiar scene.

We did not see that notable bird—though we watched with interest two tame and pretty specimens of its almost extinct species walking about in a flower-garden in the village, and superstitiously cherished there. We were told that to this day no Cornishman likes to shoot a chough or a raven. So they live and breed in peace among the twin ruins, and scream contentedly to the noisy stream which dances down the rocky hollow from

Trevena, and leaps into the sea at Porth Hern—the "iron gate," over against Tintagel. Otherwise, all is solitude and silence.

We thought we had seen everything, and come to an end, but at the hotel we found a party who had just returned from visiting some sea-caves beyond Tintagel, which they declared were "the finest things they had found in Cornwall."

It was a lovely calm day, and it was our last day. A few hours of it alone remained. Should we use them? We might never be here again. And, I think, the looser grows one's grasp of life, the greater is one's longing to make the most of it, to see all we can see of this wonderful, beautiful world. So, after a hasty meal, we found ourselves once more down at Porth Hern, seeking a boat and man—alas! not John Curgenven —under whose guidance we might brave the stormy deep.

It was indeed stormy! No sooner had we rounded the rock, than the baby waves of the tiny bay grew into hills and valleys, among which our boat went dancing up and down like a sea-gull!

"Ay, there's some sea on, there always is here, but we'll be through it presently," indifferently said the elder of the two boatmen; and plied his oars, as, I think, only these Cornish boatmen can do, talking all the while. He pointed out a slate quarry, only accessible from the sea, unless the workmen liked to be let down by ropes, which sometimes had to be done. We saw them moving about like black emmets among the clefts of the rocks, and heard plainly above the sound of the sea the click of their hammers. Strange, lonely, perilous work it must be, even in summer. In winter—

"Oh, they're used to it; we're all used to it," said our man, who was intelligent enough, though nothing equal to John Curgenven. "Many a time I've got sea-fowls' eggs on those rocks there," pointing to a cliff which did not seem to hold footing for a fly. "We all do it. The gentry buy them, and we're glad of the money. Dangerous?—yes, rather; but one must earn one's bread, and it's not so bad when you take to it young."

Nevertheless, I think I shall never look at a collection of sea-birds' eggs without a slight shudder, remembering those awful cliffs.

"Here you are, ladies, and the sea's down a bit, as I said. Hold on, mate, the boat will go right into the cave."

And before we knew what was happening, we found ourselves floated

out of daylight into darkness—very dark it seemed at first—and rocking
on a mass of heaving waters, shut in between two high walls, so narrow
that it seemed as if every heave would dash us in pieces against them;
while beyond was a dense blackness, from which one heard the beat of the
everlasting waves against a sort of tunnel, a stormy sea-grave from which
no one could ever hope to come out alive.

"I don't like this at all," said a small voice.

"Hadn't we better get out again?" practically suggested another.

But no sooner was this done than the third of the party longed to
return; and begged for "only five minutes" in that wonderful place,
compared to which Dolor Ugo, and the other Lizard caves, became as
nothing. They were beautiful, but this was terrible. Yet with its terror
was mingled an awful delight. "Give me but five, nay, two minutes more!"

"Very well, just as you choose," was the response of meek despair.
So of course, Poetry yielded. The boatmen were told to row on into
daylight and sunshine—at least as much sunshine as the gigantic overhanging
cliffs permitted. And never, never, never in this world shall I again behold
that wonderful, mysterious sea-cave.

But like all things incomplete, resigned, or lost, it has fixed itself on
my memory with an almost painful vividness. However, I promised not
to regret—not to say another word about it; and I will not. I did see it,
for just a glimpse; and that will serve.

Two more pictures remain, the last gorgeous sunset, which I watched
in quiet solitude, sitting on a tombstone by Tintagel church—a building
dating from Saxon times, perched on the very edge of a lofty cliff, and
with a sea-view that reaches from Trevose Head on one side to Bude
Haven on the other. Also, our last long dreamy drive; in the mild
September sunshine, across the twenty-one miles of sparsely inhabited
country which lie between Tintagel and Launceston. In the midst of it,
on the top of a high flat of moorland, our driver turned round and pointed
with his whip to a long low mound, faintly visible about half-a-mile off.
"There, ladies, that's King Arthur's grave."

The third, at least, that we had either seen or heard of. These
varied records of the hero's last resting-place remind one of the three heads,
said to be still extant, of Oliver Cromwell, one when he was a little boy,
one as a young man, and the third as an old man.

But after all my last and vividest recollection of King Arthur's country is that wild sail—so wild that I wished I had taken it alone—in the solitary boat, up and down the tossing waves in face of Tintagel rock ; the dark, iron-bound coast with its awful caves, the bright sunshiny land, and ever-threatening sea. Just the region, in short, which was likely to create a race like that which Arthurian legend describes, full of passionate love and deadly hate, capable of barbaric virtues, and equally barbaric crimes. An age in which the mere idea of such a hero as that ideal knight

> "Who reverenced his conscience as his God :
> Whose glory was redressing human wrong :
> Who spake no slander, no, nor listened to it :
> Who loved one only, and who clave to her—"

rises over the blackness of darkness like a morning star.

If Arthur could "come again"—perhaps in the person of one of the descendants of a prince who was not unlike him, who lived and died among us in this very nineteenth century—

> "Wearing the white flower of a blameless life—"

if this could be—what a blessing for Arthur's beloved England !

THE OLD POST-OFFICE, TREVENA.

U

L'ENVOI

WRITTEN more than a year after. The "old hen" and her chickens have long been safe at home. A dense December fog creeps in everywhere, choking and blinding, as I finish the history of those fifteen innocent days, calm as autumn, and bright as spring, when we three took our Unsentimental Journey together through Cornwall. Many a clever critic, like Sir Charles Coldstream when he looked into the crater of Vesuvius, may see "nothing in it" — a few kindly readers looking a little further, may see a little more: probably the writer only sees the whole.

But such as it is, let it stay—simple memorial of what Americans would call "a good time," the sunshine of which may cast its brightness far forward, even into that quiet time "when travelling days are done."

THE END.

APPENDIX: A Bibliographic Memoir

Notes on the life and work of Dinah Maria Muloch (Mrs. Craik)
(1826 - 1887)

The final literary contribution that the author of *John Halifax* was to make to the Victorian world of readers was an article she prepared for one of Oscar Wilde's editorial ventures, about the development of dramatic art in Britain. With less than his usual dollop of stinging wit, Wilde manages to turn his strong disagreement with both her suggested methods for controlling the then current vices of the stage, and the content of her analysis of the ills, into yet another compliment to her purity of thought and nobility of aim. The article in question had arrived with Wilde for publication only a few days before she died on October 17, 1887, and in his own *Literary and Other Notes* he mentions that she had almost completed a second, to be called "Between Schooldays and Marriage". The heavy loss to literature which Wilde records at the death of Mrs. Craik, is placed in a more realistic context for our own time by the tributes of R. Brimley Johnson in *The Women Novelists* in 1918. Some 30 years posthumously Johnson assigns her place 'in all essentials, to the modern school of novelists; although (like many another of her day) she appears almost more out-of-date than the women of genius who preceded her. For the "average" writers belong to one age and only one.'

Faint praise we may rightly call Johnson's comment, and yet we should also consider the pantheon of lady writers with whom he is comparing this good woman: those of greater genius who warrant greater mention are Fanny Burney, Jane Austen, Charlotte Bronte, George Eliot and Mrs. Gaskell, the names that every student of the novel must conjure with, male or female. Clearly, however, Johnson does not relegate Mrs. Craik to the realm of unimportance, not even to his final appendix entitled 'A List of Minor Writers', but credits her exclusively with discovering and developing the "novel for the young person." Here, and amongst the reviews of other critics earlier in this century (Henry Sidgwick, Amy Cruse, A.H. Miles, Richard Garnett) Mrs. Craik is found as a tender and sensitive writer on domestic and family concerns with a definite predisposition to moralise on personal and social responsibility. Rather than take active part in social reform movements, her message was about the personal fight, the person's energies put to the good for the benefit of others. In this effort, her ideal of manhood (or personhood) is made clear through the fine character of John Halifax. None of her other writings, numerous though they were, ever achieved the fame of this hero, though writings such as The Little Lame Prince, and poems such as *Rothesay Bay* and *Douglas, Douglas, tender and true*, are known to many who may well have forgotten (if they ever knew of) their author.

In the centenary year of her death, 1987, Lambolle House Publications (Princess House, 50 East Castle Street, London WIN 7AP) re-issued her selected fairy stories of 1863. This lovely book, so characteristic of the interests of Mrs. Craik, is now available through booksellers on order, or direct from the publishers, and is correctly entitled, *The Classic Book of Fairy Stories*.

In a Biographical Introduction to one of the many editions of *John Halifax*, the anonymous writer credits Mrs. Craik's "lifelong friend, Mrs. Oliphant with the few facts we now know about her." Otherwise, Dinah Craik is said to have lived an uneventful, contented and 'sentimental' existence amongst a large circle of friends and admirers. One suspects that our lack of knowledge of intimate details about her personal life, whatever they might have been, would perfectly please Mrs. Craik. The object of a rare attack of her vitriol was the literary biographer, or as she called this category of writer: The Literary Ghouls (essay by this title in *Studies from Life* -1861).

"The generality of female authors do not desire, living or dead, to be made into a public spectacle. Something in womanhood instinctively revolts from it- as it would from caressing its dearest friends at a railway station, or performing its toilet in the open air."

Further to a lengthy example which the reader may presume to allude the life of Elizabeth Barrett Browning (though nameless in description) Mrs. Craik concludes, "For charity's sake - for the dead woman's sake- leave the whole history untold. Cover it up! let her name and her books live, but let her life and its sorrows be heard of no more." Earlier in the same essay, she points to the only reason why she believed biographies should be written; "But let us be chronicled, not as authors, because we have written a book or so worth reading, but because we have lived a life worth remembering; the story of which will have a beneficial influence on lives yet to come....Everything that is great and noble, virtuous and heroic in any author's life - in the life of any man or woman - by all means, after a decent time has elapsed, let it be faithfully related, for the comfort, instruction, and example of later generations. The world has a right to hear and exact such chronicles of its generations gone by."

Her poems were first published in a collected volume in 1859, following a ten year period when they had been anonymously published in *Chambers' Journal*. After her marriage to George L. Craik, esq. in 1864, a copyright edition of her poems appeared (1872) with the simple re- dedication, 'To my husband', by the author of John Halifax. Having married relatively late, the Craiks were to produce no children, and it is perhaps due to this 'lack' that Dinah Craik was able to continue with her large literary output, a great deal of which was prepared for her many young friends. Little appears to be known or written about Mrs. Craik's personal life; the general impression gained from all reviewers is that there was also very little to know, since her devotion to literature was discovered early and continued in a disciplined way: carefully divided between fiction, children's books and poetry, with time spared for translations from the works of foreign friends. How she made these friends, or to what extent she travelled before and after her marriage is not specifically mentioned, except by implication from the titles and contents of her books. From these we learn that she was most certainly familiar with Scotland (1859), France (1871), Cornwall (1884) and Ireland (1887).

With the intention of launching a literary career, she had arrived in London at about the age of 20, accompanied by her mother and two younger brothers. From Mrs. Oliphant's account, we know that she settled in a small house in a side street 'a little farther off even in the wilds than ours.' This was Wildwood, North End, Hampstead, and from this "remote region near Regent's Park" she gave many small parties, and became the centre of an extensive circle of friends and influential people. Though not herself a 'bluestocking' of the time, nor an intellectual, she was widely loved for her kindness, friendliness and good intentions. Amongst her friends were Alexander Macmillan, Charles Edward Mudie and Westland Marston, and through them and Mrs. Oliphant her literary and publishing associations were numerous.

"She was a tall young woman with a slim pliant figure, and eyes that had a way of fixing the eyes of her interlocutor in a manner which did not please my shy fastidiousness. It was embarassing, as if she meant to read the other upon whom she gazed, - a pretension which one resented. It was merely, no doubt, a fashion of what was the intense school of the time. Mrs. Browning did the same thing the only time I met her, and this to one quite indisposed to be read. But Dinah was always kind, enthusiastic, somewhat didactic and apt to teach, and much looked up to by her little band of young women." (Oliphant, pp. 38-39)

It was in fact Mrs. Oliphant who introduced Mr. Blackett (of Hurst and Blackett, Publishers) at his request, to Miss Muloch, in London. The result of that meeting was the later publication of *John Halifax*, and a long publishing relationship between the two, a little to the chagrin of the 'matchmaker'. "She made a spring thus quite over my head with the helping hand of my particular friend, leaving me a little rueful, - I did not at all understand the means nor think very highly of the work, which is a thing that has happened several times, I fear, in my experience. Success as measured by money never came to my share. Miss Muloch in this way attained more with a few books, and these of very thin quality, than I with my many." (Ibid, pp. 83-84)

The seed of the story of John Halifax was said to be sown during a visit to Tewksbury in the summer of 1852, by Dinah Mulock and a friend. While walking around the Abbey and then the High Street, a sudden shower drove them into a sheltered alleyway opposite the house which she describes in the opening lines of her story. And there, she and her friend observed the scene of the boy and the loaf which she employs in the novel. The name, John Halifax, she had noted from a tombstone (now removed) in the Abbey burial ground. It is reported in another of the later Introductions to the book that she returned to Tewkesbury in 1886, the year before her death, "to be told by the landlady that the American tourist had for long made it his shrine."

After her death, some of these admirers chose to honour her memory by subscribing to the making of a marble medallion to be executed by Mr. H. H. Armstead, R.A. and placed in Tewkesbury Abbey. Tewkesbury was the stated model for Norton Bury and its surrounds form the background for the fictional events associated with John Halifax. Amongst the famous names who wished to perpetuate hers are many known to us all: Mrs. Oliphant, James Russell Lowell, Matthew Arnold, Robert Browning, and Lord Tennyson.

Melissa Hardie, Newmill, 1988

MEDALLION PORTRAIT IN THE MEMORIAL TO MRS. CRAIK IN TEWKESBURY ABBEY.

*   *   *   *   *

biographical sources

Cambridge Bibliography of English Literature (1940) Volume III, Cambridge.

Coghill, Mrs. Harry (ed.) (1899, 1974 rev.) Autobiography and Letters of Mrs. Margaret Oliphant, The Victorian Library, Leicester University Press.

Craik, Dinah Maria (1861) Studies from Life, Hurst & Blackett, London.

Cruse, Amy (1935) The Victorians and their Books, George Allen & Unwin, Ltd., London.

Dictionary of National Biography, (1917, reprint- 1973) Oxford University Press, Volume XIII.

Johnson, R. Brimley (1922) The Women Novelists, Collins Clear-Type Press, London.

Muir, Percy (1979 rev.) English Children's Books, B.T. Batsford, Ltd. London.

Shaylor, Joseph, Introduction (1898) to John Halifax, Gentleman, J.M. Dent & Co., London.

The Complete Works of Oscar Wilde (1923) Volume XII - Criticisms and Reviews, Doubleday, Page & Company, New York.

A LIST OF MRS. CRAIK'S WORKS

Cola Monti, or the Story of a Genius (1849, 1866 (revised), 1883)
The Ogilvies, A Novel (1849, 1875)
Olive (1850)
The Head of the Family (1851)
Alice Learmont, A Fairy Tale (1852; 1884 (revised)
Bread upon the Waters: a Governess's Life (1852)
Agatha's Husband, A Novel (1853)
A Hero, Philip's Book (1853)
Avillon and Other Tales (1853)
John Halifax, Gentleman (1856, Leipzig, 1857, 1859, 1898, 1900,
1902, 1906, and reprints forward)
Nothing New, Tales (1857)
A Woman's Thoughts About Women (1858)
Poems (1859, 1872- as poems by the author of John Halifax)
Romantic Tales (1859)
A Life for a Life (1859)
Domestic Stories (1860)
Our Year. A Child's Book (1860)
Studies from Life (1861)
Mistress and Maid (1862)
The Fairy Book: the Best Popular Fairy Stories selected and
rendered anew (1863, 1987-re-issued)
A New Year's Gift to Sick Children (1865)
Home Thoughts and Home Scenes (1865)
Christian's Mistake (1865)
A Noble Life (1866)
How to Win Love, or Rhoda's Lesson. A Story for the Young (1866)
Two Marriages (1867)
M. de Barante, by Guizot (translation-1867)
A French Country Family, by Mme. de Witt (translation-1867)
The Woman's Kingdom (1868)
The Unkind Word and Other Stories (1869)
A Brave Lady (1870)
A Parisian Family (translation-1870)
Fair France. Impressions of a Traveller (1871)
Little Sunshine's Holiday (1871)
Twenty Years Ago (1871)
Hannah (1872)
Adventures of a Brownie (1872)
Is It True? Tales Curious and Wonderful (1872)
An Only Sister (translation- 1873)
Songs of Our Youth (1874)
My Mother and I (1874)
Sermons Out of Church (1875)
The Little Lame Prince (1875)
The Laurel Bush (1877)
Will Denbigh, Nobleman (1877)
A Legacy (1878)
Young Mrs. Jardine (1879)
Thirty Years. Poems New and Old (1881, 1888)
Children's Poetry (1881)
His Little Mother and Other Tales (1881)
Plain Speaking (1882)
An Unsentimental Journey Through Cornwall (1884, 1988 (facsimile)
Miss Tommy (1884)
About Money and Other Things (1886)
King Arthur- not a love story (1886)
Fifty Golden Years; Incidents in the Queen's Reign (1887)
An Unknown Country (Ireland) (1887)
Concerning Men and Other Papers (1888)